The Diagnosis and Management of Depression

THE DIAGNOSIS
AND MANAGEMENT
OF DEPRESSION

AARON T. BECK, M. D.

Professor of Psychiatry
University of Pennsylvania School of Medicine;
Chief of Section, Department of Psychiatry,
Philadelphia General Hospital, Philadelphia

University of Pennsylvania Press

Philadelphia

TO PHYLLIS

Copyright © 1967, 1973 by Aaron T. Beck, M.D.
All rights reserved
Library of Congress Catalog Card Number: 73-83290
ISBN: (cloth bound edition) 0-8122-7674-4
ISBN: (paper bound edition) 0-8122-1059-X
Editorial production by *Weidner Associates, Inc.,* Cinnaminson, N.J.

Contents

Part II. TREATMENT OF DEPRESSION

Preface

Depression is the most common psychiatric disorder treated in office practice and in outpatient clinics. Some authorities have estimated that at least 12 per cent of the adult population will have an episode of depression of sufficient clinical severity to warrant treatment. Prompt diagnosis and treatment of this condition is obviously a major health concern. Several restrospective studies of suicides in England revealed that most of the patients had been seen by their family physician within a few weeks prior to the suicidal attempt, but despite the presence of telltale signs of depression, the diagnosis had generally been missed; consequently, appropriate treatment had not been instituted. It is obvious that solid information regarding the identification and management of depression is essential not only to reduce the misery caused by this condition but to reduce the incidence of suicide, one of the 10 leading causes of death in the United States.

Advances in the diagnosis and in the treatment of depression have been intimately related to each other. The recent development of sophisticated rating scales and other psychological techniques for classifying depression have provided a systematic basis for identifying types of depression and for quantifying changes. Concomitantly, the development of a variety of antidepressant agents has stimulated further modifications in the classification of depression. The most dramatic example has been the discovery that some states of excitement that would have been diagnosed previously as schizophrenia respond well to lithium and are now classified as the manic phase of manic-depressive disorder. Similarly, differences in response to electroconvulsive therapy and to some of the antidepressant drugs have provided a rationale for further subdividing depression.

Since depression is often masked by somatic complaints, its diagnosis may be missed. The presenting symptomatology of weight loss, gastrointestinal complaints, chronic fatigue, and pains in almost any part of the body may suggest a physical disorder. Much valuable time is consumed in attempts to investigate the presumed physical disorder while the patient is doomed to experience unremitting depression and may continuously hover at the brink of suicide. Even when a somatic disorder has been excluded as the source of the symptoms, the long-suffering patient may be discharged with the physician's cheery reassurance that there is nothing physically wrong with him.

In recent years, thousands of publications on the subject of depression have flooded the scientific literature. The unabridged edition of this present volume (*Depression: Causes and Treatment*) culled the voluminous literature and presented a critical review of systematic studies of all aspects of depression—classification, diagnosis, course, biological factors, psychological factors, and treatment. In addition, the various theories of depression were described and the empirical basis of these theories was reviewed.

The present abridged edition focuses on the two major problems of most practical concern to the practitioner: first, the diagnosis, classification, and clinical course of depression; secondly, the treatment modalities. Since the greatest recent advances have been relevant to the pharmacotherapy of depression, this chapter has been updated and completely rewritten. The chapter includes a comprehensive survey of the controlled studies of the treatment of depression by drugs and electroconvulsive therapy and a summary of known toxic reactions of the pharmacotherapeutic agent as well as suggestions regarding the management of side effects. It is essential, however, for the physician to keep abreast of the new information on the indications, contraindications, and toxicity published periodically by the pharmaceutical manufacturers and the Food and Drug Administration.

In addition to reviewing the literature, I have presented some of the findings of a long-term research project conducted at the University of Pennsylvania and supported in part by grants from the National Institute of Mental Health. In the course of this investigation, more than 1,000 patients were studied and considerable data were accumulated regarding the clinical and psychological aspects of depression. Additional data were collected in the course of the psychotherapy of depressed patients. The findings of these studies are included in Chapters 2 and 8.

It is my pleasure to acknowledge the contributions of Jeffrey Morris for his participation in the literature review and also to Armine Papazian for her help in copy editing. I am also grateful to Ruth Greenberg and Mary Lovell for their assistance. Finally, I am thankful to Leonette Fleming for her careful typing of the manuscript.

The author and publisher wish to express their gratitude for permission to reproduce material that originally appeared in the following publications: *Acta Psychiatrica Scandinavica*, *Archives of General Psychiatry*, and *Journal of the American Medical Association*.

AARON T. BECK, M.D.

Philadelphia, Pennsylvania

Part I.
CLINICAL ASPECTS
OF DEPRESSION

Chapter 1.
The Definition of Depression

PARADOXES OF DEPRESSION

Depression may someday be understood in terms of its paradoxes. There is, for instance, an astonishing contrast between the depressed person's image of himself and the objective facts. A wealthy man moans that he doesn't have the financial resources to feed his children. A widely acclaimed beauty begs for plastic surgery in the belief that she is ugly. An eminent physicist berates himself "for being stupid."

Despite the torment experienced as the result of these self-debasing ideas, the patients are not readily swayed by objective evidence or by logical demonstration of the irrationality of these ideas. Moreover, they often perform acts that seem to enhance their suffering. The wealthy man puts on rags and publicly humiliates himself by begging for money to support himself and his family. A clergyman with an unimpeachable reputation tries to hang himself because "I'm the world's worst sinner." A scientist whose work has been confirmed by numerous independent investigators, publicly "confesses" that his discoveries were a hoax.

Attitudes and behaviors such as these are particularly puzzling—on the surface, at least—because they seem to contradict some of the most strongly established axioms of human nature. According to the "pleasure principle," the patient should be seeking to maximize his satisfactions and minimize his pain. According to the time-honored concept of the instinct of self-preservation, he should be attempting to prolong his life rather than to terminate it.

Although depression (or melancholia) has been recognized as a clinical syndrome for over 2,000 years, as yet no completely satisfactory explanation of its puzzling and paradoxical features has been found. There are still major unresolved issues regarding its nature, its classification, and its etiology. Among these are the following:

1. Is depression an exaggeration of a mood experienced by the normal, or is it qualitatively as well as quantitatively different from a normal mood?

2. Is depression a well-defined clinical entity with a specific etiology

and a predictable onset, course, and outcome, or is it a "wastebasket" category of diverse disorders?

3. Is depression a type of reaction (Meyerian concept), or is it a disease (Kraepelinian concept)?

4. Is depression caused primarily by psychological stress and conflict, or is it related primarily to a biological derangement?

There are no universally accepted answers to these questions. In fact, there is sharp disagreement among clinicians and investigators who have written about depression. There is considerable controversy regarding the classification of depression and a few writers see no justification for using this nosological category at all. The nature and etiology of depression are subject to even more sharply divided opinion. Some authorities contend that depression is primarily a psychogenic disorder; others maintain just as firmly that it is caused by organic factors. A third group supports the concept of two different types of depression: a psychogenic type and an organic type.

The importance of depression is recognized by everyone in the field of mental health. According to Kline (1964), more human suffering has resulted from depression than from any other single disease affecting mankind. Depression is second only to schizophrenia in first and second admissions to mental hospitals in the United States, and it has been estimated that the prevalence of depression outside hospitals is five times greater than that of schizophrenia (Dunlop, 1965). A systematic survey of the prevalence of depression in a sharply defined geographical area indicated that 3.9 per cent of the population more than 20 years of age was suffering from depression at a specified time (Sørenson and Strömgren, 1961).

DESCRIPTIVE CONCEPTS OF DEPRESSION

The condition that today we label depression has been described by a number of ancient writers under the classification of "melancholia." The first clinical description of melancholia was made by Hippocrates in the fourth century B.C. He also referred to swings similar to mania and depression (Jelliffe, 1931).

Aretaeus, a physician living in the second century, A.D., described the melancholic patient as "sad, dismayed, sleepless. . . . They become thin by their agitation and loss of refreshing sleep. . . At a more advanced stage, they complain of a thousand futilities and desire death." It is noteworthy that Aretaeus specifically delineated the manic-depressive cycle. Some authorities believe that he anticipated the Kraepelinian synthesis of manic-depressive psychosis, but Jelliffe discounts this hypothesis.

Plutarch, in the second century A.D., presented a particularly vivid and detailed account of melancholia:

He looks on himself as a man whom the Gods hate and pursue with their anger. A far worse lot is before him; he dares not employ any means of averting or of remedying the evil, lest he be found fighting against the gods. The physician, the consoling friend, are driven away. 'Leave me,' says the wretched man, 'me, the impious, the accursed, hated of the gods, to suffer my punishment.' He sits out of doors, wrapped in sackcloth or in filthy rags. Ever and anon he rolls himself, naked, in the dirt confessing about this and that 'sin. He has eaten or drunk something wrong. He has gone some way or other which the Divine Being did not approve of. The festivals in honor of the gods give no pleasure to him but fill him rather with fear or a fright.*

Pinel at the beginning of the nineteenth century described melancholia as follows:

The symptoms generally comprehended by the term melancholia are taciturnity, a thoughtful pensive air, gloomy suspicions, and a love of solitude. Those traits, indeed, appear to distinguish the characters of some men otherwise in good health, and frequently in prosperous circumstances. Nothing, however, can be more hideous than the figure of a melancholic brooding over his imaginary misfortunes. If moreover possessed of power, and endowed with a perverse disposition and a sanguinary heart, the image is rendered still more repulsive.

These accounts bear a striking similarity to modern textbook descriptions of depression; they are also similar to contemporary autobiographical accounts such as that by Clifford W. Beers (1928). The cardinal signs and symptoms used today in diagnosing depression are found in the ancient descriptions: disturbed mood (sad, dismayed, futile); self-castigations ("the accursed, hated of the gods"); self-debasing behavior ("wrapped in sackcloth or dirty rags. . . he rolls himself, naked, in the dirt"); wish to die; physical and vegetative symptoms (agitation, loss of appetite and weight, sleeplessness); and delusions of having committed unpardonable sins.

The foregoing descriptions of depression include the typical characteristics of this condition. There are few psychiatric syndromes whose clinical descriptions are so constant through successive eras of history.† It is noteworthy that the historical descriptions of depression indicate that its manifestations are observable in all aspects of behavior, including the traditional psychological divisions of affection, cognition, and conation.

Because the disturbed feelings are generally a striking feature of depression, it has become customary in recent years to regard this condition as a "primary mood disorder" or as an "affective disorder." The central importance ascribed to the feeling component of depression is exemplified by the practice of utilizing affective adjective check lists to define and meas-

* Quoted by Zilboorg (1941).
† For a complete presentation of the descriptions of depression through the ages, see Robert Burton (1621).

ure depression. The representation of depression as an affective disorder is as misleading as it would be to designate scarlet fever as a "disorder of the skin" or as a "primary febrile disorder." There are many components to depression other than mood deviation. In a significant proportion of the cases, no mood abnormality at all is elicited from the patient. In our present state of knowledge, we do not know which component of the clinical picture of depression is primary, or whether they are all simply external manifestations of some unknown pathological process.

Depression may now be defined in terms of the following attributes:

1. A specific alteration in mood: sadness, loneliness, apathy.

2. A negative self-concept associated with self-reproaches and self-blame.

3. Regressive and self-punitive wishes: desires to escape, hide, or die.

4. Vegetative changes: anorexia, insomnia, loss of libido.

5. Change in activity level: retardation or agitation.

SEMANTICS OF DEPRESSION

One of the difficulties in conceptualizing depression is essentially semantic, viz., that the term has been variously applied to designate: a particular type of feeling or symptom; a symptom-complex (or syndrome); and a well-defined disease entity.

Not infrequently, normal people say they are depressed when they observe any lowering of their mood below their baseline level. A person experiencing a transient sadness or loneliness may state that he is depressed. Whether this *normal* mood is synonymous with, or even related to, the feeling experienced in the abnormal condition of depression is open to question. In any event, when a person complains of feeling inordinately dejected, hopeless, or unhappy, the term *depressed* is often used to label this subjective state.

The term depression is often used to designate a complex pattern of deviations in feelings, cognition, and behavior (described in the previous section) that is not represented as a discrete psychiatric disorder. In such instances it is regarded as a syndrome, or symptom-complex. The cluster of signs and symptoms is sometimes conceptualized as a psychopathological dimension ranging in intensity (or in degree of abnormality) from mild to severe. The syndrome of depression may at times appear as a concomitant of a definite psychiatric disorder such as schizophrenic reaction; in such a case, the diagnosis would be "schizophrenic reaction with depression." At times, the syndrome may be secondary to, or a manifestation of, organic disease of the brain such as general paresis of cerebral arteriosclerosis.

Finally, the term depression has been used to designate a discrete nosological entity. The term is generally qualified by some adjective to indicate a particular type or form, as for example: reactive depression, agitated depression, or psychotic-depressive reaction. When conceptualized as a specific clinical entity, depression is assumed to have certain consistent attributes in addition to the characteristic signs and symptoms; these attributes include a specifiable type of onset, course, duration, and outcome.

In medicine, a clinical entity or disease is assumed to be responsive to specific forms of treatment (not necessarily discovered as yet), and to have a specific etiology. There is a considerable body of evidence indicating that the clinical entity depression responds to certain drugs and/or electroconvulsive therapy (ECT), but there is no consensus as yet regarding its etiology.

DEPRESSION AND NORMAL MOODS

There is little agreement among authorities regarding the relationship of depression to the changes in mood experienced by normal individuals. The term, *mood,* is generally applied to a spectrum of feelings extending from elation and happiness at one extreme, to sadness and unhappiness at the other. The particular feelings encompassed by this term, consequently, are directly related to either happiness or sadness. Subjective states, such as anxiety or anger, that do not fit into the happiness-sadness categories are not generally included. Some authors (Hinsie and Campbell, 1960) believe that all individuals have mood-swings and that normal individuals may have "blue" hours or "blue" days. This belief has been supported by systematic studies of oscillations in mood in normal subjects (Wessman and Ricks, 1966).

The episodes of low mood or of feeling blue experienced by normal individuals are similar in a number of ways to the clinical states of depression. First, there is a similarity between the descriptions of the subjective experience of normal low mood and of depression. The words used to describe normal low mood tend to be the same used by depressives to describe their feelings—blue, sad, unhappy, empty, low, lonely. It is possible, however, that this resemblance may be due to the depressed patient's drawing on his familiar vocabulary to describe a pathological state for which he has no available words. Some patients, in fact, state that their feelings during their depressions are quite distinct from any feelings they have ever experienced when not in a clinical depression.

Second, the behavior of the depressed patient resembles that of a person who is sad or unhappy, particularly in the mournful facial expression and the lowering of the voice. Third, some of the vegetative and physical manifestations characteristic of depression are occasionally seen in individuals who are feeling sad but who would not be considered clinically depressed. A person who has failed an examination, lost a job, or been jilted, may not only feel discouraged and forlorn, but may experience anorexia, insomnia, and fatigability. Finally, many individuals experience blue states that seem to oscillate in a consistent or rhythmic fashion, independently of external stimuli, suggestive of the rhythmic variations in the intensity of depression (Wessman and Ricks, 1966).

The resemblance between depression and the low mood of normals has led to the concept that the pathological is simply an exaggeration of the normal. On the surface, this view seems plausible. As will be discussed in Chapter 2, each symptom of depression may be graded in intensity along a dimension, and the more mild intensities are certainly similar to the phenomena observed in normal individuals who are feeling blue.

In rebuttal to this *continuity hypothesis*, it could be contended that many pathological states that seem to be on a continuum with the normal state are different in their essential character from the normal state. To illustrate this, an analogy may be made between the deviations of mood and deviations of internal body temperature. While pronounced changes in body temperature are on the same continuum as are normal temperatures, the underlying factors producing the large deviations are not an extension of the normal state of health: A person may have a disease, e.g., typhoid fever, that is manifested by a serial progression in temperature and yet is categorically different from the normal state. Similarly, the deviation in mood found in depression may be the manifestation of a disease process that is distinct from the normal state.

There is no general consensus among the authorities regarding the relation of depression to normal mood swings. Some writers, notably Kraepelin and his followers, consider depression a well-defined disease, quite distinct from normal mood. They postulate the presence of a profound biological derangement as the key factor in depression. This concept of a dichotomy between health and disease is generally shared by the *somatogenic school*. The *environmentalists* seem to favor the continuity hypothesis. In their view, there is a continuous series of mood reactions ranging from a normal reaction to an extreme reaction in a particularly susceptible person. The psychobiological school founded by Adolph Meyer tends to favor this view.

The ultimate answer to the question as to whether there is a dichotomy or continuity between normal mood and depression will have to wait until the question of the etiology of depression is fully resolved.

Chapter 2.
Symptomatology of Depression

PREVIOUS SYSTEMATIC STUDIES

As stated in Chapter 1, there has been remarkable consistency in the descriptions of depression since ancient times. While there has been unanimity among the writers on many of the characteristics, however, there has been lack of agreement on many others. The core signs and symptoms such as low mood, pessimism, self-criticism, and retardation or agitation seem to have been universally accepted. Other signs and symptoms that have been regarded as intrinsic to the depressive syndrome include autonomic symptoms, constipation, difficulty in concentrating, slow thinking, and anxiety. Campbell (1953), e.g., listed 29 medical manifestations of autonomic disturbance, among which the most common in manic depressives were hot flashes, tachycardia, dyspnea, weakness, head pains, coldness and numbness of the extremities, frontal headaches, and dizziness.

There have been very few systematic studies designed to delineate the characteristic signs and symptoms of depression. Cassidy, Flanagan, and Spellman (1957) compared the symptomatology of 100 patients diagnosed as manic depressive with a control group of 50 patients with diagnoses of recognized medical diseases. The frequency of the specific symptoms was determined by having the patient complete a questionnaire of 199 items. Among the symptoms that were endorsed significantly more often by those in the psychiatric group were anorexia, sleep disturbance, low mood, suicidal thoughts, crying, irritability, fear of losing the mind, poor concentration, and delusions.

It is interesting to note that Cassidy and his coworkers found that only 25 per cent of the manic-depressive group thought that they would get well as compared with 61 per cent of those who were medically ill. This is indicative of the pessimism which is characteristic of manic depressives: Almost all could be expected to recover completely from their illness, in contrast to the number of incurably ill among the medical patients. Certain symptoms sometimes attributed to manic depressives, such as constipation, were found in similar proportions in the two groups.

Campbell reported a high frequency of medical symptoms, generally attributed to autonomic imbalance, among manic depressives. Cassidy's study, however, found that most of these medical symptoms occurred at least as frequently among the medically ill patients as among the manic-depressive patients. Moreover, many of these symptoms were found in a group of healthy control patients. Headaches, for instance, were reported by 49 per cent of the manic-depressive patients, 36 per cent of the medically sick controls, and 25 per cent of the healthy controls. When the symptoms of manic depressives, anxiety neurotics, and hysteria patients were compared, it was found that autonomic symptoms occurred at least as frequently in the latter two groups as they did in the manic-depressive group. Palpitation, for instance, was reported by 56 per cent of the manic depressives, 94 per cent of the anxiety neurotics, and 76 per cent of the hysterics. It therefore seems clear that autonomic symptoms are not specifically characteristic of manic-depressive disorders.

Recent systematic investigations of the symptomatology of depressive disorders have been conducted to delineate the typical clinical picture, as well as to suggest typical subgroupings of depression (Grinker *et al.*, 1961; Friedman *et al.*, 1963). A major problem in interpreting the findings of these investigations is presented by the fact that the case material consisted primarily of depressed patients and did not include a control group of nondepressed psychiatric patients for comparison. It is not possible, therefore, to determine which symptom clusters might be characteristic of depression or its various subgroupings, and which might occur in any psychiatric patient or even in normals.

In this chapter, following a review of the chief complaints, the symptoms of depression are described under four major headings: emotional; cognitive; motivational; and physical and vegetative. This is followed by a section on delusions and hallucinations. Some of these divisions may appear arbitrary, and it is undoubtedly true that some of the symptoms described separately may simply be different facets of the same phenomenon. Nonetheless, I think it is desirable at this stage to present the symptomatology as broadly as possible, despite the inevitable overlap. Following the symptoms, a section on behavioral observation has been included. The descriptions in this latter section were obtained by direct observation of the patients' nonverbal as well as their verbal behavior.

CHIEF COMPLAINT

The chief complaint presented by depressed patients often points immediately to the diagnosis of depression; on the other hand, it sometimes suggests a physical disturbance. Skillful questioning can generally determine whether the basic depressive symptomatology is present.

The chief complaint may take a variety of forms: (*1*) an unpleasant emotional state; (*2*) a changed attitude towards life; (*3*) somatic symptoms of a specifically depressive nature; or (*4*) somatic symptoms not typical of depression.

Among the most common subjective complaints (Lewis, 1934) are: "I feel miserable." "I just feel hopeless." "I'm desperate." "I'm worried about everything." Although depression is generally considered an affective disorder, it should be emphasized that a subjective change in mood is not reported by all depressed patients. As in many other disorders, the absence of a significant clinical feature does not rule out the diagnosis of that disorder. In our series, for instance, only 53 per cent of the mildly depressed patients acknowledged feeling sad or unhappy.

Sometimes the chief complaint is in the form of a change of one's actions, reactions, or attitudes towards life. For example, a patient may say, "I don't have any goals any more." "I don't care anymore what happens to me." "I don't see any point to living." Sometimes the major complaint is a sense of futility about life.

Often the chief complaint of the depressed patient centers around some physical symptom that is characteristic of depression. The patient may complain that he gets tired easily, that he has no pep, or that he has lost his appetite. Sometimes he complains of some alteration in his appearance or in his bodily functions. Women complain that they are beginning to look old or are getting ugly. Other patients complain of some dramatic physical symptom such as, "My bowels are blocked up."

Depressed patients attending medical clinics or consulting either internists or general practitioners frequently present some symptom suggestive of a physical disease (Watts, 1957). In many cases, the physical examination fails to reveal any physical abnormality. In other cases, some minor abnormality may be found but it is of insufficient severity to account for the magnitude of the patient's discomfort. On further examination, the patient may acknowledge a change in mood but is likely to attribute this to his somatic symptoms.

Severe localized pain or generalized pain may often be the chief focus of a patient's complaint. Bradley (1963) reported 35 cases of depression in which the main complaint was severe, localized pain. In each case, feelings of depression were either spontaneously reported by the patient or were elicited on interview. In those cases in which the pain was integrally connected with the depression, the pain cleared up as the depression cleared up. Kennedy (1944) and Von Hagen (1957) reported that pain associated with depression responded to electroconvulsive therapy (ECT).

In the study by Cassidy, Flanagan, and Spellman (1957), an analysis was made of the chief complaints of the manic-depressive patients. These complaints were divided into several categories which included (*1*) psychological; (*2*) localized medical; (*3*) generalized medical; (*4*) mixed medical and psychological; (5) medical, general and local; and (6) no clear information. Some of the typical complaints in each category are listed below:

(1) *Psychological* (*58 per cent*): "depressed;" "I have nothing to look forward to;" "afraid to be alone;" "no interest;" "can't remember anything," "get discouraged and hurt;" "black moods and blind rages;" "I'm doing such stupid things;" "I'm all mixed up;" "very unhappy at times;" "brooded around the house."

(2) *Localized medical* (*18 per cent*): "head is heavy," "pressure in my throat;" "headaches;" "urinating frequently;" "pain in head like a balloon that burst;" "upset stomach."

(3) *Generalized medical* (*11 per cent*): "tired;" "I'm exhausted;" "I feel all in;" "tire easy;" "jumpy most at night;" "I can't do my work, I don't feel strong;" "I tremble like a leaf."

(4) *Medical and psychological* (*2 per cent*): "I get scared to death and can't breathe;" "stiff neck and crying spells."

(5) *Medical, general and local* (*2 per cent*): "breathing difficulty . . . pain all over;" "I have no power. My arms are weak." "I can't work."

(6) *No information* (*9 per cent*).

The authors tabulated the percentages of the various symptom types which were named by the manic-depressive patients and by the medically sick controls (Table 2–1). It is worthy of note that a medical symptom, either localized or generalized, was reported by 33 per cent of the manic-depressive patients and by 92 per cent of the medically sick controls.

SYMPTOMS

The decision as to which symptoms should be included here was made as the result of several steps: First, several textbooks of psychiatry and monographs on depression were studied to determine what symptoms have been attributed to depression by general consensus. Second, in an intensive study of 50 depressed patients and 30 nondepressed patients in psychotherapy, I attempted to tally which symptoms occurred significantly more often in the depressed than in the nondepressed group. On the basis of this tabulation, an inventory consisting of items relevant to depression was constructed and pretested on approximately 100 patients. Finally, this inventory was revised and presented to 966 psychiatric patients. Distributions of the symptoms reported in response to the inventory are presented in Tables 2–3 through 2–7.

One of the symptoms, namely *irritability*, did not occur significantly more frequently in the depressed than in the nondepressed patients. It, therefore, has been dropped from the list. Incidentally, Cassidy and his coworkers (1957) found that this symptom was more frequent in the anxiety-neurotic group than in the manic-depressive group.

Table 2–1.
CHIEF COMPLAINTS OF 100 PATIENTS WITH MANIC-DEPRESSIVE
DIAGNOSIS AND 50 PATIENTS WITH MEDICAL DIAGNOSIS*

Type of complaint	Manic depressive (%)	Medical controls (%)
Psychological	58	0
Medical, localized	18	86
Medical, generalized	11	6
Medical, localized and generalized	2	0
Medical and psychological	2	6
No information	9	2

* Adapted from Cassidy, Flanagan, and Spellman, 1957.

Some of the symptoms often attributed to the manic-depressive syndrome are not included in the symptom descriptions in this chapter. For instance, *fear of death* was not included because it was not found to be any more common among the depressed patients than among the non-depressed in the preliminary clinical study. Cassidy, Flanagan, and Spellman found, in fact, that fear of death occurred in 42 per cent of patients with anxiety neurosis and only 35 per cent of the manic depressives. Similarly, constipation occurred in 60 per cent of the manic-depressive patients and 54 per cent of the patients with hysteria. Consequently, this particular symptom does not seem to be specific to depression.

Conventional nosological categories were not used in our analyses of the symptomatology. Instead of being classified according to their primary diagnoses, such as manic-depressive reaction, schizophrenia, anxiety reaction, etc., the patients were categorized according to the depth of depression which they exhibited, independently of their primary diagnoses. There were two major reasons for this. (1) In our own studies as well as in previous studies, it was found that the degree of interjudge reliability was relatively low in diagnoses made according to the standard nomenclature. Consequently, any findings based on diagnoses of such low reliability would be of relatively dubious value. The interpsychiatrist ratings of the depth of depression, on the other hand, showed a relatively high correlation (.87). (2) We found that the cluster of symptoms generally regarded as constituting the depressive syndrome occurs not only in disorders such as neurotic-depressive reaction and manic-depressive reaction, but also in patients whose primary diagnosis is anxiety reaction, schizophrenia, obsessional neurosis, etc. In fact, we have found that a patient with the primary diagnosis of one of the typical depressive categories may be less depressed than a patient whose primary diagnosis is schizophrenia, obsessional neurosis, etc. The sample, therefore, was divided into four groups according to the depth of depression: none, mild, moderate, and severe.

In addition to making the usual qualitative distinctions among the symptoms, I have attempted to provide a guide for assessing their severity. The symptoms are discussed in terms of how they are likely to appear in the mild, moderate, and severe states (or phases) of depression. This may serve as an aid to the clinician or investigator in making a quantitative estimate of the severity of depression. The tables may be used as a guide in diagnosing depression since they show the relative frequency of the symptoms in patients who were considered to be either nondepressed, mildly depressed, moderately depressed, or severely depressed.

The description of the patient sample is found in Table 2–2.

EMOTIONAL MANIFESTATIONS

The term *emotional manifestations* refers to the changes in the patient's feelings or the changes in his overt behavior *directly* attributable to his feeling states (Table 2–3). In assessing emotional manifestations, it is important to take into account the individual's premorbid mood level and behavior, as well as what the examiner might consider the *normal* range in the patient's particular age, sex, and social group. The occurrence of frequent crying spells in a patient who rarely or never cried before becoming depressed might indicate a greater level of depression than it would in a patient who habitually cried whether depressed or not.

Dejected Mood

The characteristic depression in mood is described differently by various clinically depressed patients. Whatever term the patient uses to describe

Table 2–2.

DISTRIBUTION OF PATIENTS ACCORDING TO RACE, SEX, AND DEPTH OF DEPRESSION

Race and sex of patient	Depth of depression				
	None	*Mild*	*Moderate*	*Severe*	*Total*
White males	71	98	91	15	275
White females	51	90	137	40	318
Negro males	50	32	30	4	116
Negro females	52	77	102	26	257
Total Whites	122	188	228	55	593
Total Negroes	102	109	132	30	373
Total males	121	130	121	19	391
Total females	103	167	239	66	575
TOTAL	224	297	360	85	966

Table 2–3.

EMOTIONAL MANIFESTATIONS: FREQUENCY AMONG DEPRESSED AND
NONDEPRESSED PATIENTS

	Depth of depression			
	None (%) (n=224)	Mild (%) (n=288)	Moderate (%) (n=377)	Severe (%) (n=86)
Dejected mood	23	50	75	88
Self-dislike	37	64	81	86
Loss of gratification	35	65	86	92
Loss of attachments	16	37	60	64
Crying spells	29	44	63	83
Loss of mirth response	8	29	41	52

n = No. of patients.

his subjective feelings should be further explored by the examiner. If the patient uses the word "depressed," for instance, the examiner should not take the word at its face value but should try to determine its connotation for the patient. Persons who are in no way clinically depressed may use this adjective to designate transient feelings of loneliness, boredom, or discouragement.

Sometimes the feeling is expressed predominantly in somatic terms, such as "a lump in my throat," or "I have an empty feeling in my stomach," or "I have a sad, heavy feeling in my chest." On further investigation, these feelings generally are found to be similar to the feelings expressed by other patients in terms of adjectives such as sad, unhappy, lonely, or bored.

The intensity of the mood deviation must be gauged by the examiner. Some of the rough criteria of the degree of depression are the relative degree of morbidity implied by the adjective chosen, the qualification by adverbs such as "slightly" or "very," and the degree of tolerance the patient expresses for the feeling (e.g., "I feel so miserable I can't stand it another minute.").

Among the adjectives used by depressed patients in answer to the question, "How do you feel?" are the following: miserable, hopeless, blue, sad, lonely, unhappy, downhearted, humiliated, ashamed, worried, useless, guilty. Eighty-eight per cent of the severely depressed patients reported some degree of sadness or unhappiness, as compared with 23 per cent of the nondepressed patients.

Mild: The patient indicates he feels blue or sad. The unpleasant feeling tends to fluctuate considerably during the day and at times may be absent, and the patient may even feel cheerful. Also the dysphoric feeling can be relieved partially or completely by outside stimuli, such as a compliment, a joke, or a favorable event. With a little effort or ingenuity the examiner can usually evoke a positive response. Patients at this level generally react with genuine amusement to jokes or humorous anecdotes.

Moderate: The dysphoria tends to be more pronounced and more persistent. The patient's feeling is less likely to be influenced by other people's attempts to cheer him up, and any relief of this nature is temporary. Also, a diurnal variation is frequently present: The dysphoria is often worse in the morning and tends to be alleviated as the day progresses.

Severe: In cases of severe depression, the patient is apt to state he feels "hopeless" or "miserable." Agitated patients frequently state they are "worried." In our series, 70 per cent of the severely depressed patients indicated that they were sad all the time and "could not snap out of it," that they were so sad that it was very painful; or that they were so sad they could not stand it.

Negative Feelings Toward Self

Depressed patients often express negative feelings about themselves. These feelings may be related to the general dysphoric feelings just described, but they are different in that they are specifically directed toward the self. The patients appear to distinguish feelings of dislike for themselves from negative attitudes about themselves such as, "I am worthless." The frequency of self-dislike ranged from 37 per cent in the nondepressed group to 86 per cent among the severely depressed.

Mild: The patient states that he feels disappointed in himself. This feeling is accompanied by ideas such as: "I've let everybody down . . . If I had tried harder, I could have made the grade."

Moderate: The feeling of self-dislike is stronger and may progress to a feeling of disgust with himself. This is generally accompanied by ideas such as: "I'm a weakling . . . I don't do anything right . . . I'm no good."

Severe: The feeling may progress to the point where the patient hates himself. This stage may be identified by statements such as: "I'm a terrible person . . . I don't deserve to live . . . I'm despicable . . . I loathe myself."

Reduction in Gratification

The loss of gratification is such a pervasive process among depressives that many patients regard it as the central feature of their illness. In our series, 92 per cent of the severely depressed patients reported at least partial loss of satisfaction; this was the most common symptom among the depressed group as a whole.

Loss of gratification appears to start with a few activities and, as the depression progresses, spreads to practically everything the patient does. Even activities that are generally associated with biological needs or drives, such as eating or sexual experiences, are not spared. Experiences that are primarily psychosocial such as achieving fame, receiving expressions of love or friendship, or even engaging in conversations, are similarly stripped of their pleasurable properties.

The emphasis placed by some of the patients on loss of satisfaction gives the impression that they are especially oriented in their lives toward obtaining gratification. Whether or not this applies to the premorbid state cannot be stated with certainty, but it is true that in their manic states the feverish pursuit of gratification is a cardinal feature.

The initial loss of satisfaction from activities involving responsibility or obligation, such as those involved in the role of worker, housewife, or student, is often compensated for by increasing satisfaction from recreational activities. This observation has prompted Saul (1947) and others to suggest that, in depression, the "give-get" balance is upset; the patient, depleted psychologically over a period of time by activities predominantly *giving* in nature, experiences an accentuation of his passive needs, which are gratified by activities involving less of a sense of duty or responsibility (giving) and more of a tangible and easily obtained satisfaction. In the more advanced stages of the illness, however, even passive, regressive activities fail to bring any satisfaction.

Mild: The patient complains that some of the joy has gone out of his life. He no longer gets a "kick" or pleasure from his family, friends, or job. Characteristically, activities involving responsibility, obligation, or effort become less satisfying to him. Often, he finds greater satisfaction from *passive* activities involving recreation, relaxation, or rest. He may seek unusual types of activities in order to get some of his former thrill. One patient reported that he could always pull himself out of a mild depression by watching a performance of deviant sexual practices.

Moderate: He feels bored much of the time. He may try to enjoy some of his former favorite activities but they seem "flat" to him now. Business or professional activities which formerly excited him now fail to move him. He may obtain temporary relief from a change, such as a vacation, but the boredom returns upon resumption of his usual activities.

Severe: He experiences no enjoyment from activities that were formerly pleasurable. He may even feel an aversion for activities he once enjoyed. Popular acclaim or expressions of love or friendship no longer bring any degree of satisfaction. The patients almost uniformly complain that nothing gives them any degree of satisfaction.

Loss of Emotional Attachments

Loss of emotional involvement in other people or activities usually accompanies loss of satisfaction. This is manifested by a decline in his degree of interest in particular activities or in his affection or concern for other persons. Loss of affection for members of his family is often a cause for concern to the patient and occasionally is a major factor in his seeking medical attention. Sixty-four per cent of the severely depressed patients reported loss of feeling for or interest in other people, whereas only 16 per cent of the nondepressed patients reported this symptom.

Mild: In mild cases, there is some decline in the degree of enthusiasm for, or absorption in, an activity. The patient sometimes reports that he does not experience the same intensity of love or affection for his spouse, children, or friends. On the other hand, he may feel more dependent on them.

Moderate: The loss of interest or of positive feeling may progress to indifference. A number of patients described this as a "wall" between themselves and other people. Sometimes a husband may complain that he no longer loves his wife, or a mother may be concerned that she does not seem to care about her children or what happens to them. A previously devoted employee may report he is no longer concerned about his job. A woman may no longer care about her appearance.

Severe: Loss of attachment to external objects may progress to apathy. The patient may not only lose any positive feeling for members of his family, but may be surprised to find that his only reaction is a negative one. In some cases, the patient experiences only a kind of cold hate which may be masked by dependency. A typical patient's report is, "I've been told I have love and can love. But now I don't feel anything toward my family. I don't give a damn about them. I know this is terrible, but sometimes I hate them."

Crying Spells

Increased periods of crying are frequent among depressed patients. This is particularly true of the depressed women in our series. Of the severely-depressed patients, 83 per cent reported that they cried more frequently than they did before becoming depressed, or that thy felt like crying even though the tears did not come.

Some patients who rarely cried when not depressed were able to diagnose the onset of depression by observing a strong desire to weep. One woman remarked, "I don't know whether I feel sad or not but I do feel like crying so I guess I am depressed." Further questioning elicited the rest of the cardinal symptoms of depression.

Mild: There is an increased tendency to weep or cry. Stimuli or situations that would ordinarily not affect the patient may now elicit tears. A mother, for example, might burst out crying during an argument with her children or if she feels her husband is not attentive. Although increased crying is frequent among mildly depressed women, it is unusual for a mildly depressed man to cry (Lewis, 1934).

Moderate: The patient may cry during the psychiatric interview, and references to his problems may elicit tears. Men who have not cried since childhood may cry while discussing their problems. Women patients may cry for no apparent reason: "It just comes over me like a wave and I can't help crying." Sometimes the patient feels relieved after crying but more often he feels more depressed.

Severe: By the time he has reached the severe stage, a patient who was easily moved to tears in the earlier phase may find that he no longer can cry even when he wants to. He may weep, but he has no tears ("dry depression"). Twenty-nine per cent of the severely depressed patients reported that although they had previously been capable of crying when feeling sad, they no longer could cry—even though they wanted to do so.

Loss of Mirth Response

Depressed patients frequently volunteer the information that they have lost their sense of humor. The problem does not seem to be loss of the ability to perceive the point of the joke or even, when instructed, to construct a joke. The difficulty rather seems to be that the patient does not respond to humor in the usual way. He is not amused, does not feel like laughing, and does not get any feeling of satisfaction from a jesting remark, joke, or cartoon.

In our series, 52 per cent of the severely depressed patients indicated that they had lost their sense of humor, as contrasted with 8 per cent of the nondepressed patients.

Nussbaum and Michaux (1963) studied the response to humor (in the form of riddles and jokes) in 18 women patients with severe neurotic and psychotic depressions. They found that improvements in response to humorous stimuli correlated well with clinical ratings of improvement of the depression.

Mild: Patients who frequently enjoy listening to jokes and telling jokes find that this is no longer such a ready source of gratification. They remark that jokes no longer seem funny to them. Furthermore, they do not handle kidding or joshing by their friends as well as previously.

Moderate: The patient may see the point of a joke and can even force a smile, but he is usually not amused. He cannot see the light side of events and tends to take everything seriously.

Severe: The patient does not respond at all to humorous sallies by other people. Where others may respond to the humorous element in a joke he is more likely to respond to the aggressive or hostile content and feel hurt or disgusted.

COGNITIVE MANIFESTATIONS

The cognitive manifestations of depression include a number of diverse phenomena (Table 2–4). One group is composed of the patient's distorted

Table 2–4.

COGNITIVE MOTIVATIONAL MANIFESTATIONS: FREQUENCY AMONG
DEPRESSED AND NONDEPRESSED PATIENTS

	Depth of depression			
Manifestation	*None* (%) (n=224)	*Mild* (%) (n=288)	*Moderate* (%) (n=377)	*Severe* (%) (n=86)
Low self-evaluation	38	60	78	81
Negative expectation	22	55	72	87
Self-blame and self-criticism	43	67	80	80
Indecisiveness	23	48	67	76
Distorted self-image	12	33	50	66
Loss of motivation	33	65	83	86
Suicidal wishes	12	31	53	74

n = No. of patients.

attitudes toward himself, his experience, and his future. This group includes low self-evaluations, distortions of the body image, and negative expectations. Another symptom, self-blame, expresses the patient's notion of causality: He is prone to hold himself responsible for any difficulties or problems that he encounters. A third kind of symptom involves the area of decision-making: The patient typically vacillates and is indecisive.

Low Self-Evaluation

Low self-esteem is a characteristic feature of depression. Self-devaluation is apparently part of the depressed patient's pattern of viewing himself as deficient in those attributes that are specifically important to him: ability, performance, intelligence, health, strength, personal attractiveness, popularity, or financial resources. Often the sense of deficiency is expressed in terms such as "I am inferior" or "I am inadequate." This symptom was reported by 81 per cent of the severely depressed patients and by 38 per cent of the nondepressed patients.

The sense of deficiency may also be reflected in complaints of deprivation of love or material possessions. This reaction is most apparent in patients who have had, respectively, an unhappy love affair or a financial reversal just prior to the depression.

Mild: The patient shows an excessive reaction to any of his errors or difficulties and is prone to regard them as a reflection of his inadequacy or as a defect in himself. He makes comparisons with other people and, more often than not, concludes he is inferior. It is possible, however, to correct his inaccurate self-evaluations, at least temporarily, by confronting him with appropriate evidence or by reasoning with him.

Moderate: Most of the patient's thought content revolves about his sense of deficiency, and he is prone to interpret neutral situations as indicative of this deficiency. He exaggerates the degree and significance of any errors. When he looks at his present and past life, he sees his failures as outstanding and his successes as faint by comparison. He complains that he has lost confidence in himself and his sense of inadequacy is such that when confronted with tasks he has easily handled in the past, his initial reaction is "I can't do it."

The religious or moralistic patient tends to dwell on his sins or moral shortcomings. The patient who placed a premium on his personal attractiveness, intelligence, or business success tends to believe that he has slipped in these areas. Attempts to modify his distorted self-evaluations by reassuring the patient or by presenting contradictory evidence generally meets with considerable resistance; any increase in realistic thinking about himself is transient.

Severe: The patient's self-evaluations are at the lowest point. He drastically downgrades himself in terms of his personal attributes and his role as parent, spouse, employer, etc. He regards himself as worthless, completely inept, and a total failure. He claims that he is a burden to members of his family and that they would be better off without him. He may be preoccupied with ideas that he is the world's worst sinner, completely impoverished, or totally inadequate. Attempts to correct his erroneous ideas are generally fruitless.

Negative Expectations

A gloomy outlook and pessimism are closely related to the feelings of hopelessness mentioned previously. More than 78 per cent of the depressed patients reported a negative outlook, as compared with 22 per cent of the nondepressed group. This symptom showed the highest correlation with the clinical rating of depression.

The patient's pattern of expecting the worst and rejecting the possibility of any improvement poses formidable obstacles in attempts to engage him in a therapeutic program. His negative outlook is often a source of frustration to his friends, family, and physician when they try to help him. Not infrequently, for example, a patient may discard his antidepressant pills because he believes *a priori* that they "cannot do him good."

Unlike the anxious patient, who tempers his negative anticipations with the realization that the unpleasant events may be avoided or will pass in time, the depressed patient thinks in terms of a future in which his present deficient condition (financial, social, physical) will continue or will even get worse. This sense of permanence and irreversibility of his status or problems seems to form the basis for his consideration of suicide as a logical course of action. The relationship of hopelessness to suicide is indicated by the finding that, of all the symptoms that were correlated with suicide, the correlation coefficient of hopelessness: suicide was the highest.

Mild: The patient tends to expect a negative outcome in ambiguous or equivocal situations. When his associates and friends feel justified in anticipating favorable results, his expectations lean toward the negative or pessimistic. Whether the subject of his concern is his health, or his personal problems, or his economic problems, he has doubts as to whether any improvement will take place.

Moderate: He regards the future as unpromising and states he has nothing to which he can look forward. It is difficult to get him to do anything because his initial response is, "I won't like it" or "it won't do any good."

Severe: He views the future as black and hopeless. He states that he will never get over his troubles and that things cannot get better for him. He believes that none of his problems can be solved. The patient makes statements such as: "This is the end of the road. From now on I will look older and uglier." "There is nothing here for me any more. I have no place. There is no future." "I know I can't get better . . . It's all over for me."

Self-Blame and Self-Criticism

The depressive's perseverating self-blame and self-criticism appear to be related to his egocentric notions of causality and his penchant for criticizing himself for his alleged deficiencies. He is particularly prone to ascribe adverse occurrences to some deficiency in himself, and then to rebuke himself for having this alleged defect. In the more severe cases, the patient may blame himself for happenings that are in no way connected with him and abuse himself in a savage manner. Eighty per cent of the severely depressed patients reported this symptom.

Mild: In mild cases, the patient is prone to blame and criticize himself when he falls short of his rigid, perfectionist standards. If people seem less responsive to him, or he is slow at solving a problem, he is likely to berate himself for being dull or stupid. He seems to be intolerant of any shortcomings in himself and cannot accept the idea that it is human to err.

Moderate: The patient is likely to criticize himself harshly for any aspects of his personality or behavior which he judges to be substandard. He is likely to blame himself for mishaps that are obviously not his fault. His self-criticisms become more extreme.

Severe: In the severe state, the patient is even more extreme in his use of self-blame or self-criticism. He makes statements such as, "I'm responsible for the violence and suffering in the world. There's no way in which I can be punished enough for my sins. I wish you would take me out and hang me." He views himself as a social leper or criminal, and interprets various extraneous stimuli as signs of public disapproval.

Indecisiveness

Difficulty in making decisions, vacillating between alternatives, and changing decisions are depressive characteristics that are usually quite vexing to the patient's family and friends as well as to the patient himself. The frequency of indecisiveness ranged from 48 per cent in the mildly depressed patients to 76 per cent in the severely depressed group.

There appear to be at least two facets to this indecisiveness. The first is primarily in the cognitive sphere. The patient anticipates making the wrong decision: Each time he considers one of the various possibilities he tends to regard it as wrong and to think that he will regret making that choice. The second facet is primarily motivational and is related to "paralysis of the will," avoidance tendencies, and increased dependency. The patient has a lack of motivation to go through the mental operations that are required to arrive at a conclusion. Also, the idea of making a decision represents a burden to him; he desires to evade, or at least to get help with any situation that he perceives will be burdensome. Furthermore, he realizes that making a decision often commits him to a course of action and, since he desires to avoid action, he is prone to procrastinate.

Routine decisions which must be made in carrying out their occupational roles become major problems for the depressed patients. A professor could not decide what material to include in a lecture; a housewife could not decide what to cook for an evening meal; a student could not decide whether to spend the spring recess studying at college or whether to go home; an executive could not decide whether to hire a new secretary.

Mild: A patient who can ordinarily make rapid-fire decisions finds that solutions do not seem to occur to him so readily. Where in his normal state he reaches a decision "without even thinking about it," he now finds himself impelled to mull over the particular problem, review the possible consequences of the decision, and consider a variety of often irrelevant alternatives. His fear of making the wrong decision is reflected in a general sense of uncertainty. Frequently, he seeks confirmation from another person.

Moderate: Difficulty in making decisions spreads to almost every activity and involves such minor problems as what clothes to wear, what route to take to the office, and whether to have a haircut. Often it is of little practical importance which alternative is selected, but the vacillation and failure to arrive at some decision can have unfavorable consequences. A woman, for example, spent several weeks trying to choose between two shades of paint for her house. The two shades under consideration were hardly distinguishable, but her failure to reach a decision created a turmoil in the house, the painter having left his buckets of paint and scaffolding until a decision could be made.

Severe: The severely depressed patients generally believe they are incapable of making a decision and, consequently, do not even try. When a housewife was prodded to make a shopping list or a list of clothes for her children to take to camp, she insisted she could not decide what to put down. The patient frequently has doubts about everything he does and says. One woman seriously doubted that she had given her correct name to the psychiatrist, or that she had enunciated it properly.

Distortion of Body Image

The patient's distorted picture of his physical appearance is often quite marked in depression. This occurs somewhat more frequently among women than among men. In our series, 66 per cent of the severely depressed patients believed that they had become unattractive, as compared with 12 per cent of the nondepressed patients.

Mild: The patient begins to be excessively concerned with his physical appearance. A woman finds herself frowning at her reflection whenever she passes a mirror. She examines her face minutely for signs of blemishes. She becomes preoccupied with the thought that she looks plain or is getting fat.

Moderate: The concern about physical appearance is greater. The patient believes that there has been a change in his looks since the onset of the depression even though there is no objective evidence to support this idea. When he sees an ugly person, he thinks, "I look like that." As he becomes worried about his appearance, his brow becomes furrowed. When he observes his furrowed brow in the mirror, he thinks, "my whole face is wrinkled and the wrinkles will never disappear." Some patients seek plastic surgery to remedy the fancied or exaggerated facial changes.

Sometimes, the patient may believe that he has grown fat even though there is no objective evidence to support this. In fact, some patients have this notion even though they are losing weight.

Severe: The idea of personal unattractiveness becomes more fixed. The patient believes that he is ugly and repulsive looking. He expects other people to turn away from him in revulsion: One woman wore a veil and another turned her head whenever anybody approached her.

MOTIVATIONAL MANIFESTATIONS

Motivational manifestations include consciously experienced strivings, desires, and impulses that are prominent in depressions. These motivational patterns can often be inferred from observings the patient's behavior; however, direct questioning generally elicits a fairly precise and comprehensive description of his motivations (see Table 2–4).

A striking feature of the characteristic motivations of the depressed patient is their *regressive* nature. The term regressive is applicable in that the patient seems drawn to activities that are the least demanding for him either in terms of the degree of responsibility or initiative required, or the amount of energy to be expended. He turns away from activities that are specifically associated with the adult role and seeks activities that are more characteristic of the child's role. When confronted with a choice, he prefers passivity to activity and dependence to independence (autonomy); he avoids responsibility and escapes from his problems rather than trying to solve them; he seeks immediate, but transient, gratifications instead of delayed, but prolonged, satisfactions. The ultimate manifestation of the escapist trend is expressed in his desire to withdraw from life via suicide.

An important aspect of these motivations is that their fulfillment is generally incompatible with the individual's major premorbid goals and values. In essence, yielding to his passive impulses and his desires to retreat or commit suicide leads to abandonment of his family, friends, and vocation. Similarly, he defaults his chance to obtain personal satisfaction through accomplishments or interpersonal relations. By avoiding even the simplest problems, moreover, he finds that they accumulate until they seem overwhelming to him.

The specific motivational patterns to be described are presented as distinct phenomena although they are obviously interrelated and may, in fact, represent different facets of the same fundamental pattern. It is possible that certain phenomena are primary and the others are secondary or tertiary; for instance, it could be postulated that paralysis of the will is the result of escapist or passive wishes, a sense of futility, loss of external investments, or the sense of fatigue. Since these suggestions are purely speculative, it seems preferable at present to treat these phenomena separately, rather than prematurely to assign primacy to certain patterns.

Paralysis of the Will

The loss of positive motivation is often a striking feature of depression. The patient may have a major problem in mobilizing himself to perform even the most elemental and vital tasks such as eating, elimination, or taking medication to relieve his distress. The essence of the problem appears to be that, although he can define for himself what he should do, he does not experience any internal stimulus to do it. Even when urged, cajoled, or threatened, he does not seem able to arouse any desire to do these things. Loss of positive motivation ranged from 65 per cent of the mild cases to 86 per cent of the severe cases.

Occasionally an actual or impending shift in a patient's life situation may serve to mobilize his constructive motivations. One notably retarded and apathetic patient was suddenly aroused when her husband became ill and she experienced a strong desire to help him. Another patient experienced a return of positive motivation when informed she was going to be hospitalized, a prospect she viewed as extremely distasteful.

Mild: The patient finds that he no longer spontaneously desires to do certain specific things, especially those that do not bring any immediate gratification. An advertising executive observes a loss of drive and initiative in planning a special sales promotion; a college professor finds himself devoid of any desire to prepare his lectures; a medical student loses his desire to study. A housewife, who formerly felt driven to engage in a variety of domestic and community projects, described her loss of motivation in the following terms: "I have no desire to do anything. I just do things mechanically without any feeling for what I'm doing. I just go through the motions like a robot and when I run down I just stop."

Moderate: In moderate cases the loss of spontaneous desire spreads to almost all of the patient's usual activities. A woman complained, "There are certain things I know I have to do like eat, brush my teeth, and go to the bathroom, but I have no desire to do them." In contrast to the severely depressed patient, the moderately depressed patient finds he can "force" himself to do things. Also, he is responsive to pressure from other people or to potentially embarrassing situations. A woman, for instance, waited in front of an elevator for about 15 minutes because she could not mobilize any desire to press the button. When others approached the elevator, however, she rapidly pressed the button lest they think she was peculiar.

Severe: In severe cases, there often is complete paralysis of the will. The patient has no desire to do anything, even those things that are essential to life. Consequently, he may be relatively immobile unless prodded or pushed into activity by others. It is sometimes necessary to pull the patient out of bed, wash, dress, and feed him. In extreme cases, even communication may be blocked by the patient's inertia. One woman, who was unable to respond to questions during the worst part of her depression, remarked later that even though she "wanted" to answer she could not summon the "will power" to do so.

Avoidance, Escapist, and Withdrawal Wishes*

The wish to break out of the usual pattern or routine of life is a common manifestation of depression. The clerk wants to get away from his paper work, the student daydreams of faraway places, and the housewife yearns to leave her domestic duties. The depressed individual regards his duties as dull, meaningless, or burdensome and wants to escape to an activity that offers relaxation or refuge.

---

* This symptom had not been included in the inventory administered to the patients; hence, there are no data available regarding its relative frequency. On the basis of clinical observation, I believe it is a frequent symptom.

These escapist wishes resemble the attitudes described as paralysis of the will. A useful distinction is that the escapist wishes are experienced as definite motivations with specific goals, whereas paralysis of the will refers to the loss or absence of motivation.

Mild: The mildly depressed patient experiences a strong inclination to avoid or to postpone doing certain things that he regards as uninteresting or taxing. He tends to shy away from attending to details that he considers to be unimportant. He is likely to procrastinate or avoid entirely an activity that does not promise immediate gratification or which involves effort. Just as he is repelled by activities that involve effort or responsibility, he is attracted to more passive and less complex activities.

A depressed student expressed this as follows: "It's much easier to daydream in lectures than pay attention. It's easier to stay home and drink than call a girl for a date. . . . It's easier to mumble and not be heard than to talk clearly and distinctly. It's much easier to write sloppily than to make the effort to write legibly. It's much easier to lead a self-centered, passive life than to make the effort to change it."

Moderate: In moderate cases, avoidance wishes are stronger and spread to a much wider range of his usual activities. A depressed college professor described this as follows: "Escape seems to be my strongest desire. I feel as though I would feel better in almost any other occupation or profession. As I ride the bus to the university, I wish I were the bus driver instead of a teacher."

The patient thinks continually of ways of diversion or escape. He would like to indulge in passive recreation such as going to the movies, watching television, or getting drunk. He daydreams of going to a desert island or of becoming a hobo. At this stage, he may withdraw from most social contacts since interpersonal relations seem to be too demanding. At the same time, because of his loneliness and increased dependency, he may want to be with other people.

Severe: In severe cases, the wish to avoid or escape is manifested in marked seclusiveness. Not infrequently the patient stays in bed, and when people approach, he may hide under the covers. A patient said, "I just feel like getting away from everybody and everything. I don't want to see anybody or do anything. All I want to do is sleep." One form of escape that generally occurs to the severely depressed patient is suicide. The patient feels a strong desire to end his life as a way of escaping from a situation he regards as intolerable.

Suicidal Wishes

Suicidal wishes have historically been associated with a depressed state. While suicidal wishes may occur in nondepressed individuals, they occur substantially more frequently in depressed patients. In our series this was the symptom reported least frequently (12 per cent) by the nondepressed patients, but it was reported frequently (74 per cent) by the severely depressed patients. This difference indicates the diagnostic value of this particular symptom in the identification of severe depression. The intensity with which this symptom was expressed also showed one of the highest correlations with the intensity of depression.

The patient's interest in suicide may take a variety of forms. It may be experienced as a passive wish ("I wish I were dead"); an active wish ("I want to kill myself"); as a repetitive, obsessive thought without any volitional quality; as a daydream; or as a meticulously conceived plan. In some patients, the suicidal wishes occur constantly throughout the illness and the patient may have to battle continually to ward them off. In other cases, the wish is sporadic and is characterized by a gradual build-up, then a slackening of intensity until it disappears temporarily. Patients often report, once the wish has been dissipated, that they are glad they did not succumb to it. It should be noted that the impulsive suicidal attempt may be just as dangerous as the deliberately planned attempt.

The importance of suicidal symptoms is obvious, since nowadays it is practically the only feature of depression that poses a reasonably high probability of fatal consequences. The incidence of suicide among manic depressives ranged from 2.8 per cent in one study with a 10-year follow-up (Stenstedt, 1952) to 5 per cent in a 25-year period of observation (Rennie, 1942).

Mild: Wishes to die were reported by about 31 per cent of the mildly depressed patients. Often these take the passive form such as, "I would be better off dead." Although the patient states he would not do anything to hasten his death, he may find the idea of dying attractive. One patient looked forward to an airplane trip because of the possibility the plane might crash.

Sometimes, the patient expresses an indifference towards living ("I don't care whether I live or die."). Other patients may show an ambivalence ("I would like to die but at the same time I'm afraid of dying.").

Moderate: In these cases, suicidal wishes are more direct, frequent, and compelling; there is a definite risk of either impulsive or premeditated suicidal attempts. The patient may express his desire in the passive form: "I hope I won't wake up in the morning;" or, "If I died, my family would be better off." The active expression of the wish may vary from ambivalent statement, "I'd like to kill myself but I don't have the guts," to the bald assertion, "If I could do it and not botch it up, I would go ahead and kill myself." The suicidal wish may be manifested by the patient's taking unnecessary risks. A number of patients drove their cars at excessive rates of speed in the hope that something might happen.

Severe: In severe cases, suicidal wishes tend to be intense although the patient may be too retarded to complete a suicidal attempt Among the typical statements are the following: "I feel so hopeless. Why won't you let me die." "It's no use. All is lost. There is only one way out—to kill myself." "I must weep myself to death. I can't live and you won't let me die." "I can't bear to live through another day. Please put me out of my misery."

Increased Dependency*

The term dependency is used here to designate the *desire* to receive help, guidance, or direction rather than the actual process of relying on someone else. The accentuated wishes for dependency have only occasionally been included in clinical descriptions of depression; they have, however, been recognized and assigned a major etiological role in several psychodynamic explanations of depression (Abraham, 1911; Rado, 1928). The accentuated orality attributed to depressed patients by those authors includes the kinds of wishes that are generally regarded as "dependent."

Since increased dependency has been attributed to other conditions as well as to depression, the question could be raised whether dependency can be justifiably listed as a *specific* manifestation of depression. Increased-dependency wishes are seen in an overt form in people who have an acute or chronic physical illness; moreover, covert or repressed dependency has been regarded by many theoreticians as the central factor in certain psychosomatic conditions such as peptic ulcer, as well as in alcoholism and other addictions. However, it is my contention that frank, undisguised, and intensified desires for help, support, and encouragement are very prominent elements in the advanced stages of depression and belong in any clinical description of this syndrome. In other conditions, intensified dependency may be a variable and transient characteristic.

The desire for help seems to transcend the realistic *need* for help, i.e., the patient can often reach his objective without assistance. Receiving help, however, appears to carry special emotional meaning for the patient beyond its practical importance and is often satisfying—at least temporarily.

Mild: The patient who is ordinarily very self-sufficient and independent begins to express a desire to be helped, guided, or supported. A patient, for instance, who always had insisted on driving when he was in the car with his wife, asked her to drive. He felt that he was capable of driving, but the idea of her driving was more appealing to him at this time.

As the dependency wishes become stronger, they tend to supersede the individual's habitual independent drives. He now finds that he prefers to have somebody do things with him rather than do them alone. The dependent desire does not seem to be simply a by-product of the feelings of helplessness and inadequacy or fatigue. The patient feels a craving for help

---

* In our study, the degree of dependency motivation was not included in the inventory.

even though he recognizes that he does not need it and when the help is received, he generally experiences some gratification and lessening of his depression.

Moderate: The patient's desire to have things done for him, to receive instruction and reassurance is stronger. The patient who experiences a wish for help in the mild phase now experiences this as a *need*. Receiving help no longer is an optional luxury but is now conceived of as a necessity. A depressed woman, who was legally separated from her husband, begged him to come back to her. "I need you deseperately," she said. It was not clear to her exactly what she needed him for, except that she wanted to have a strong person near her.

When confronted with a task or problem, the moderately depressed patient feels impelled to seek help before attempting to undertake it himself. He not infrequently states that he wants to be told what to do. Some patients shop around for opinions about a certain course of action and seem to be more involved in the idea of getting advice than in using it. One woman would ask numerous questions about trivial problems but did not seem to pay much attention to the content of the answer—just so an answer was forthcoming.

Severe: The intensity of the desire to be helped is increased and the content of the wish has a predominantly passive cast. It is couched almost exclusively in terms of wanting someone to do everything for the patient and to take care of him. The patient is no longer concerned about getting direction or advice, or in sharing problems. He wants the other person to do the job and to solve the problem for him. A patient clung to the physician and pleaded, "Doctor, you must help me." Her desire was for the psychiatrist to do everything for her without her doing anything. She even wanted the psychiatrist to adopt her children.

The patient may show his dependency by not wanting to leave the doctor's office or not wanting him to leave. Terminating the interview often becomes a difficult and painful process.

Table 2–5.

INTERCORRELATION OF PHYSICAL AND VEGETATIVE
SYMPTOMS ($n=606$)*

Symptom	*Fatigue*	*Loss of sleep*	*Loss of appetite*	*Loss of libido*
Depth of depression	.31	.30	.35	.27
Fatigability		.25	.20	.29
Sleep disturbance			.35	.29
Loss of appetite				.33

n = No. of patients.
* Pearson product-moment correlation coefficients.

Table 2–6.

VEGETATIVE AND PHYSICAL MANIFESTATIONS: INCIDENCE AMONG
DEPRESSED AND NONDEPRESSED PATIENTS

	Degree of depression			
Manifestation	None (%) (n=224)	Mild (%) (n=288)	Moderate (%) (n=377)	Severe (%) (n=86)
Loss of appetite	21	40	54	72
Sleep disturbance	40	60	76	87
Loss of libido	27	38	58	61
Fatigability	40	62	80	78

n = No. of patients.

VEGETATIVE AND PHYSICAL MANIFESTATIONS

The physical and vegetative manifestations are considered by some authors to be evidence for a basic autonomic or hypothalamic disturbance that is responsible for the depressive state (Campbell, 1953; Kraines; 1957). These symptoms, contrary to expectation, have a relatively low correlation with each other and with clinical ratings of the depth of depression. The intercorrelation matrix is shown in Table 2–5. The frequency of the symptoms among depressed and nondepressed patients is shown in Table 2–6.

Loss of Appetite

For many patients, loss of appetite is often the first sign of an incipient depression and return of appetite may be the first sign that it is beginning to lift. Some degree of appetite loss was reported by 72 per cent of the severely depressed patients and only 21 per cent of the nondepressed patients.

Mild: The patient may find that he no longer eats his meals with the customary degree of relish or enjoyment. There is also some dulling of his desire for food.

Moderate: The desire for food mostly may be gone and the patient may miss a meal without realizing it.

Severe: The patient may have to force himself—or be forced—to eat. There may even be an aversion for food. After several weeks of severe depression, the amount of weight loss may be considerable.

Sleep Disturbance

Difficulty in sleeping is one of the most notable symptoms of depression, although it occurs in a large proportion of nondepressed patients as well. Eighty-seven per cent of the severely depressed patients reported some interference with sleep. Difficulty in sleeping was reported by 40 per cent of the nondepressed patients.

There have been a number of careful studies of the sleep of depressed patients. The investigators have presented solid evidence, based on direct observation of the patients and EEG recordings during the night, that depressed patients sleep less than do normal controls. In addition, the studies show an excessive degree of restlessness and movement during the night among the depressed patients.

Mild: The patient reports waking a few minutes to half an hour earlier than usual. In many cases, the patient may state that, although ordinarily he sleeps soundly until awakened by the alarm clock, he now awakens several minutes before the alarm goes off. In some cases, the sleep disturbance is in the reverse direction: The patient finds that he sleeps more than usual.

Moderate: The patient awakens one or two hours earlier than usual. He frequently reports that his sleep is not restful. Moreover, he seems to spend a greater proportion of the time in light sleep. He also may awaken after three or four hours of sleep and require a hypnotic to return to sleep. In some cases, the patient manifests an excessive sleeping tendency and may sleep up to twelve hours a day.

Severe: The patient frequently awakens after only four or five hours of sleep and finds it impossible to return to sleep. In some cases, the patients claim that they have not slept at all during the night; they state that they can remember "thinking" continuously during the night. It is likely, however, as Oswald *et al.* (1963) point out, that the patients are actually in a light sleep for a good part of the time.

Loss of Libido

Some loss of interest in sex, whether of an auto-erotic or heterosexual nature, was reported by 61 per cent of the depressed patients and by 27 per cent of the nondepressed patients. Loss of libido correlated most highly with loss of appetite, loss of interest in other people, and depressed mood (see Appendix).

Mild: There is generally a slight loss of spontaneous sexual desire and of responsiveness to sexual stimuli. In some cases, however, sexual desire seems to be heightened when the patient is mildly depressed.

Moderate: Sexual desire is markedly reduced and is aroused only with considerable stimulation.

Severe: Any responsiveness to sexual stimuli is lost and the patient may have a pronounced aversion for sex.

Fatigability

Increased tiredness was reported by 79 per cent of the depressed patients and only 33 per cent of the nondepressed. Some patients appear to experience this symptom as a purely physical phenomenon: The limbs feel heavy or the body feels as though it is weighted down. Others express fatigability as a loss of "pep" or energy. The patient complains of feeling "listless," "worn out," "too weak to move," or "run down."

It is sometimes difficult to distinguish fatigability from loss of motivation and avoidance wishes. It is interesting to note that fatigability correlates more highly with lack of satisfaction (.36) and with pessimistic outlook (.36) than with other physical or vegetative symptoms such as loss of appetite (.20) and sleep disturbance (.28). The correlation with lack of satisfaction and pessimistic outlook suggests that the mental set may be a major factor in the patient's feeling of tiredness; the converse, of course, should be considered as a possibility, viz., that tiredness influences the mental set.

Some authors have conceptualized depression as a "depletion syndrome" because of the prominence of fatigability; they postulate that the patient exhausts his available energy during the period prior to the onset of the depression and that the depressed state represents a kind of hibernation, during which the patient gradually builds up a new store of energy. Sometimes the fatigue is attributed to the sleep disturbance. Against this theory is the observation that even when the patients do get more sleep as a result of hypnotics, there is rarely any improvement in the feeling of fatigue. It is interesting to note, furthermore, that the correlation between sleep disturbance and fatigability is only .28. If the sleep disturbance were a major factor, a substantially higher correlation would be expected. Fatigability may be a manifestation of loss of positive motivation.

There tends to be a diurnal variation in fatigability parallel to low mood and negative expectations. The patient tends to feel more tired upon awakening, but somewhat less tired as the day progresses.

Mild: The patient finds that he tires more easily than usual. If he has had a hypomanic period just prior to the depression, the contrast is marked: Whereas previously he could be very active for many hours without any feeling of tiredness, he now feels fatigued after a relatively short period of work. Not infrequently a diversion or a short nap may restore a feeling of vitality, but the improvement is transient.

Moderate: The patient is generally tired when he awakens in the morning. Almost any activity seems to accentuate his tiredness. Rest, relaxation, and recreation do not appear to alleviate this feeling and may, in fact, aggravate it. A patient who customarily walked great distances when well would feel exhausted after short walks when depressed. Not only physical activity, but focused mental activity, such as reading, often increases the sense of tiredness.

Severe: The patient complains that he is too tired to do anything. Under external pressure he is sometimes able to perform tasks requiring a large expenditure of energy. Without such external stimulation, however, he does not seem to be able to mobilize his energy to perform even simple tasks such as dressing himself. He may complain, for instance, that he does not have enough strength even to lift his arm.

DELUSIONS

Delusions in depression may be grouped into several categories: delusions of worthlessness; delusions of the "unpardonable" sin and of being punished or expecting punishment; nihilistic delusions; somatic delusions; and delusions of poverty. Any of the cognitive distortions described above may progress in intensity and achieve sufficient rigidity to warrant its being considered a delusion. A person with low self-esteem, for instance, may progress in his thinking to believe that he is the devil. A person with a tendency to blame himself may eventually begin to ascribe to himself certain crimes such as the assassination of the President.

To determine the frequency of the various delusions among psychotically depressed patients, a series of 280 psychotic patients were interviewed. The results are shown in Table 2–7.

Delusions of Worthlessness

Delusions of worthlessness occurred in 48 per cent of the severely depressed psychotics. This delusion was expressed in the following way by one patient: "I must weep myself to death. I cannot live. I cannot die. I have failed so. It would be better if I had not been born. My life has always been a burden. . . . I am the most inferior person in the world. . . . I am subhuman." Another patient said, "I am totally useless. I can't do anything. I have never done anything worthwhile."

Crime and Punishment

The patient believes he has committed a terrible crime for which he deserves or expects to be punished. Forty-six per cent of the severely-depressed, psychotic patients reported the delusion of being very bad sinners. In many cases, the patient feels that severe punishment such as torture or hanging is imminent. Forty-two per cent of the severely depressed patients expected punishment of some type. Many other patients believed that they were being punished and that the hospital was a kind of penal

Table 2–7.

FREQUENCY OF DELUSIONS WITH DEPRESSIVE CONTENT AMONG PSYCHOTIC
PATIENTS VARYING IN DEPTH OF DEPRESSION (*n*=280)

Delusion	*Depth of depression*			
	None (%) (n=85)	*Mild (%)* (n=68)	*Moderate (%)* (n=77)	*Severe (%)* (n=50)
Worthless	6	9	21	48
Sinner	11	19	29	46
Devil	3	4	3	14
Punishment	18	21	18	42
Dead	0	2	3	10
Body decaying	9	13	16	24
Fatal illness	5	6	14	20

n=No. of patients.

institution. The patient wails, "Will God never give up?" "Why must I be singled out for punishment?" "My heart is gone. Can't He see this? Can't He let me alone?" In some cases the patient may believe that he is the devil; 14 per cent of the severely depressed psychotics had this delusion.

Nihilistic Delusions

Nihilistic delusions have traditionally been associated with depression. A typical nihilistic delusion is reflected in the following statement: "It's no use. All is lost. The world is empty. Everybody died last night." Sometimes the patient believes that he himself is dead; this occurred in 10 per cent of the severely depressed patients.

Organ preoccupation is particularly common in nihilistic delusions. The patients complain that an organ is missing or that all their viscera have been removed. This was expressed in statements such as "My heart, my liver, my intestines are gone. I'm nothing but an empty shell."

Somatic Delusions

The patient believes that his body is deteriorating, or that he has some incurable disease. Twenty-four per cent of the severely depressed believed that their bodies were decaying. Twenty per cent believed that they had fatal illnesses. Somatic delusions are expressed in statements such as the following: "I can't eat. The taste in my mouth is terrible. My guts are diseased. They can't digest the food." "I can't think. My brain is all blocked up." "My intestines are blocked. The food can't get through." Allied to the idea of having a severe abnormality is a patient's statement, "I haven't slept at all in six months."

Delusions of Poverty

Delusions of poverty seem to be an outgrowth of the overconcern with finances manifested by depressed patients. A wealthy patient may complain bitterly, "All my money is gone. What will I live on? Who will buy food for my children?" Many authors have described the incongruity of a man of means who, dressed in rags, goes begging for alms or food.

In our study, delusions of poverty were not investigated. Because of the very high proportion of low-income patients in the series, it was difficult to distinguish a delusion of poverty from actual poverty.

In Rennie's study (1942), nearly half of the 99 cases had delusions as part of their psychoses. Forty-nine patients had ideas of persecution or of passivity. (The number of persons with each of these delusions is not given.) Typical depressive delusions were found in 25 patients: These dealt predominantly with self-blame and self-depreciation and with ideas of being dead, of their bodies being changed, or of immortality. Delusions were most common in the oldest age group (72 per cent). In patients more than 50 the content revolved predominantly around ideas of poverty, of being destroyed or tortured in some horrible manner, of being poisoned, or of being contaminated by feces.

HALLUCINATIONS

Rennie found that 25 per cent of the patients had hallucinations. This was most prominent in the recurrent depressive group. Samples of the types of hallucinations were as follows: "I conversed with God." "I heard the sentence, 'Your daughter is dead'." "I heard people talking through my stomach." "I saw a star on Christmas day." "I saw and heard my dead mother." "Voices told me not to eat." "Voices told me to walk backward." "Saw and heard God and angels." "Saw dead father." "Animal faces in the food." "Saw and heard animals." "Saw dead people." "Heard brother's and dead people's voices." "Saw husband in his coffin." "A voice said, 'Do not stay with your husband'." "Saw snakes and Negroes." "Saw two men digging a grave."

In our study, we found that 13 per cent of the severely depressed, psychotic patients acknowledged hearing voices that condemned them. This was the most frequent type of hallucination reported.

CLINICAL EXAMINATION

APPEARANCE

The psychiatrists in our study made ratings of the intensity of certain clinical features in the depressed and nondepressed patients. Many of these

Table 2–8.

FREQUENCY OF CLINICAL FEATURES OF PATIENTS VARYING IN
DEPTH OF DEPRESSION ($n=486$)

Clinical feature	Depth of depression			
	None (%)	Mild (%)	Moderate (%)	Severe (%)
Sad facies	18	72	94	98
Stooped posture	6	32	70	87
Crying in interview	3	11	29	28
Speech: slow, etc.	25	53	72	75
Low mood	16	72	94	94
Diurnal variation of mood	6	13	37	37
Suicidal wishes	13	47	73	94
Indecisiveness	18	42	68	83
Hopelessness	14	58	85	86
Feeling inadequate	25	56	75	90
Conscious guilt	27	46	64	60
Loss of interest	14	56	83	92
Loss of motivation	23	54	88	88
Fatigability	39	62	89	84
Sleep disturbance	31	55	73	88
Loss of appetite	17	33	61	88
Constipation	19	26	38	52

$n=$ No. of patients.

features would be considered *signs*; i.e., they are abstracted from observable behaviors rather than from the patients' self-descriptions. Other features were evaluated on the basis of the patients' verbal reports as well as on the observation of their behavior. Some of the clinical features overlap those described in the previous section. This particular study provides an opportunity to compare the frequency of symptoms elicited in response to the inventory with the frequency of symptoms derived from a clinical examination.

The sample consisted of the last 486 patients of the 966 patients previously described in Table 2–2. The distribution of the clinical features among the nondepressed, mildly depressed, moderately depressed, and severely depressed are found in Table 2–8.

Most cases of depression can be diagnosed by inspection (Lehmann, 1959). The sad, melancholic expression combined with either retardation or agitation are practically pathognomonic of depression. On the other hand, many patients conceal their unpleasant feelings behind a cheerful facade ("smiling depression") and it may require careful interviewing to bring out a pained facial expression.

The facies show typical characteristics that are associated with sadness. The corners of the mouth are turned down, the brow is furrowed, the lines and wrinkles are deepened, and the eyes are often red from crying.

Among the descriptions used by clinicians are glum, forlorn, gloomy, dejected, unsmiling, solemn, wearily resigned (Lewis, 1934). Lewis reported weeping occurred in most of the women, but in only one-sixth of the men in his sample.

In severe cases, the facies may appear to be frozen in a gloomy expression. Most patients, however, show some lability of expression, especially when their attention is diverted away from their feelings. Genuine smiles may be elicited at times even in the severe cases, but they are generally transient. Some patients present a forced or social smile, which may be deceiving. The so-called mirthless smile, which indicates a lack of any genuine amusement, is easily recognized. This type of smile may be elicited in response to a humorous remark by the examiner and indicates the patient's intellectual awareness of the humor but without any emotional response to it.

A sad facies was observed in 85 per cent of the depressed group (including mild, moderate, and severe cases) and in 18 per cent of the non-depressed group. In the severely depressed group, 98 per cent showed this characteristic.

RETARDATION

The most striking sign of a retarded depression is reduction in spontaneous activity. The patient tends to stay in one position longer than usual and to use a minimum of gestures. His movements are slow and deliberate as though his body and limbs are weighted down. He walks slowly, frequently hunched over, and with a shuffling gait. These postural characteristics were observed in 87 per cent of the severely depressed patients in our sample.

The speech shows decreased spontaneity and the verbal output is reduced. The patient does not initiate a conversation or volunteer statements and, when questioned, responds in a few words. Sometimes, speaking is decreased only when a painful subject is being discussed. The pitch of the patient's voice is often lowered and he tends to speak in a monotone. These vocal characteristics were observed in 75 per cent of the severely depressed patients.

The more retarded patients may start sentences but not complete them. They may answer questions with grunts or groans. The most severe cases may be mute. As Lewis points out, it is sometimes difficult to distinguish the scanty talk of a depressive from that of a well-preserved, suspicious, paranoid schizophrenic. In both conditions, there may be pauses, hesitations, evasion, breaking-off, and brevity. The diagnosis must rest on other observations—of content and behavior.

In severe depressions the patient may manifest signs of a syndrome that has been labelled *stupor* or *semi-stupor* (Hoch, 1921). If left alone, he may remain practically motionless whether standing, sitting, or lying in bed. There is rarely, if ever, any waxy flexibility as seen in catatonia or any apparent clouding of consciousness. The patients vary in the degree to which they respond to stimulation. Some respond to sustained efforts by the examiner to establish rapport; others appear oblivious. I questioned several patients in the latter category after they recovered from their depression and they reported that they had experienced feelings and thoughts during clinical examination but had felt incapable of expressing them in any way.

In extreme cases, the patient does not eat or drink even with urging. Food placed in his mouth may remain there until removed and under such circumstances tube feeding becomes necessary as a life-preserving measure. Sometimes, the patient does not move his bowels and digital removal of feces or enemas are necessary. Saliva accumulates and drools out of his mouth. He blinks infrequently and may develop corneal ulcers.

Bleuler (1911, p. 209) described the melancholic triad consisting of depressive affect, inhibition of action, and inhibition of thinking. The first two characteristics are certainly typical of retarded depression. There is, however, a strong question as to whether there is an inhibition of the thought process. Lewis (1934) believes that thinking is active—or even hyperactive—even though speech is inhibited. Refined psychological tests, furthermore, have failed to show significant interference with thought processes.

Agitation

The chief characteristic of the agitated patient is his ceaseless activity. He cannot sit still but moves about constantly in the chair. He conveys a sense of restlessness and disturbance in wringing his hands or handkerchief, tearing his clothing, picking at his skin, and clenching and unclenching his fingers. He may rub his scalp or other parts of his body until the skin is worn away.

He may get out of his chair many times in the course of an interview and pace the floor. At night, he may get out of bed frequently and walk incessantly back and forth. It is just as difficult for him to engage in constructive activity as it is for him to stay still. His agitation is also manifested by frequent moans and groans. He approaches the doctors, nurses, and other patients and besieges them with requests or pleas for reassurance.

The emotions of frenzy and anguish are congruent with his thought content. He wails, "Why did I do it. Oh, God, what is to become of me. Please have mercy on me." He believes that he is about to be butchered or buried alive. He moans, "My bowels are gone. It's intolerable." He screams. "I can't stand the pain. Please put me out of my misery." He groans, "My home is gone. My family is gone. I just want to die. Please let me die."

The thought content of the retarded patient appears to revolve around passive resignation to his fate. The agitated patient, on the other hand, cannot accept or tolerate the torture he envisions. The agitated behavior appears to represent desperate attempts to fight off his impending doom.

Chapter 3.
Course and Prognosis

DEPRESSION AS A CLINICAL ENTITY

In the previous chapter, depression was treated as a psychopathological dimension or syndrome. The clinical features of depression were examined in cross-section, i.e., in terms of the cluster of pathological phenomena exhibited at a given point in time. In this chapter, depression is treated as a discrete clinical entity (such as manic-depressive reaction or neurotic-depressive reaction) that has certain specific characteristics occurring over time: in terms of onset, recovery, and recurrence. As a clinical entity or reaction type, depression has many salient characteristics that distinguish it from other clinical types such as schizophrenia, even though these other types may have depressive elements associated with them. The depressive constellation as a concomitant of other nosological entities will not be described in this chapter but will be considered later in terms of its association with schizophrenic symptomatology in the schizo-affective category.

Among the important characteristics of the clinical entity of depression are the following: There is generally a well-defined onset, a progression in the severity of the symptoms until the condition bottoms out, and then a steady regression (improvement) of the symptoms until the episode is over; the remissions are spontaneous; there is a tendency toward recurrence; the intervals between attacks are free of depressive symptoms.

IMPORTANCE OF COURSE AND OUTCOME

The longitudinal aspects of depression have been the subject of many investigations since the time of Kraepelin. Adequate information regarding the short-term and long-term course of depression is important, not only for practical management, but also for an understanding of the psychopathology, and for evaluation of specific forms of treatment. Considerable data on the life histories of depressed patients were accumulated before the advent of the specific therapeutic agents—electroconvulsive therapy (ECT) and drugs. These data are generally regarded as reflecting the natural history of the disorder, although it is difficult to separate out the effects of hospitalization.

The physician charged with making a determination of the prognosis in a given case is confronted with a number of questions.

1. In the case of a first episode of depression, what are the prospects for complete recovery, and what is the likelihood of residual symptoms or of a chronic, unrecovered state?

2. What is the probable duration of the first attack?

3. What is the likelihood of recurrence, and what is the probable duration of any multiple attacks?

4. How long must one wait following a patient's recovery from a given attack before ruling out the likelihood of recurrence?

5. What is the risk of death through suicide?

Answers to these questions can be provided by reference to cases diagnosed as manic-depressive psychoses. A number of fairly well-designed studies have been conducted to determine the fate of such patients. It should be emphasized that the available data applies primarily to hospitalized patients.

In the case of affective disorders other than manic depressive, the available data is either too unreliable or too scanty to allow definite conclusions. The diagnosis of involutional melancholia is subject to so much variation that the findings of any particular study cannot be generalized in any scientific sense. A particular sample diagnosed as involutional depression at one hospital would inevitably include a high proportion of cases that would be diagnosed as manic depressive or schizophrenic at hospitals deemphasizing the use of the label of involutional melancholia.

It is even more difficult to arrive at any conclusions regarding the duration, outcome, and relapse rate of the newer splinter groups, such as neurotic-depressive reactions and psychotic-depressive reactions. There are several reasons for this. First, since these nosological categories have come into use only recently, there has not been sufficient time for long-term observation. Second, the preponderance of the neurotic-depressive cases have been treated in private practice or in outpatient clinics; statistical surveys are more difficult to carry out under such circumstances. Third, since most patients in these two groups have received modern psychiatric management—psychotherapy, drugs, or electroconvulsive therapy—it is difficult to picture clearly the spontaneous ebb and flow of these conditions. It will probably be possible to obtain some relevant data from drug studies using a group of such patients as placebo-controls. A series described by Paskind as "manic depressive" in 1930 undoubtedly contained a preponderance of cases that would currently be diagnosed as "neurotic-depressive reactions." Since this study antedated the modern somatic therapies, the findings may be assumed to be relevant to the natural history of neurotic-depressive reactions.

SYSTEMATIC STUDIES

Kraepelin (1913) studied the general course of 899 cases of manic-depressive psychosis. The period of observation varied considerably; some patients were followed for brief periods and others for as long as 40 years. Moreover, since the follow-up depended largely on readmission to the hospital, the information on patients who were not readmitted is scanty. Despite these limitations, his study is of great value in providing solid facts regarding recurrent episodes, frequency and duration of the attacks, and duration of the intervals between attacks.

His sample is as follows: single depression, 263; recurrent depression, 177; biphasic* single episode, 106; combined, recurrent, 214; single manic episode, 102; and recurrent manic, 47.

A study of Paskind (1929, 1930a, 1930b) of cases of depression seen in private practice presents the most complete data available on the course of depressions observed outside the hospital. Although there are many serious methodological deficiencies in this study, the data presented are relevant to milder episodes of depression. Paskind reviewed the records of 633 cases of depression in the private practice of Dr. Q. T. Patrick. Although all of these cases had been placed in the all-inclusive category of manic-depressive psychosis, a review of the case histories presented in the articles leaves little doubt that these cases would be diagnosed as neurotic-depressive reactions according to the new nomenclature. In reviewing the tabulated data presented by the author, it is apparent that his findings are based on 248 cases abstracted from the original group. The cases were collected over a period of 32 years, but there is no mention of the average period of observation nor of any systematic attempt to obtain follow-up material on these patients. Paskind noted that 88 cases (32 per cent of the 248) could be classified as "brief attacks of manic-depressive psychosis," since the average duration of the episodes ranged from a few hours to a few days.

Paskind describes the symptoms of the short attacks as being exactly like those of longer attacks: profound sadness and unhappiness without obvious cause; self-reproach; self-blame; self-derogation; lack of initiative;

---

* The term biphasic is used to denote cases in which both manic and depressive episodes occurred. These cases have been designated by a variety of terms: compound, mixed, combined, double-form, cyclothymic, and cyclical. The alternating and circular types refer to cases in which one phase follows immediately after the opposite phase without any free interval. The "closed circular type" refers to uninterrupted cycles of manic and depressive phases.

lack of response to usual interests accompanied by a keen awareness of this lack; avoidance of friends; a feeling of hopelessness; death wishes; and inclinations or desire to commit suicide. Paskind states that the well-known antidotes for depression, such as a philosophic outlook, the company of friends, amusements, diversions, rest, change of scene, and good news do not cause the attacks to disappear. "Instead one finds a person in a normal mood who without apparent cause becomes within a brief period profoundly sad and unhappy; in spite of all attempts to cheer him, the attack remains for from a few hours to a few days; when it does disappear it does so as abruptly and mysteriously as it came."

Rennie (1942) did a follow-up study of 208 patients with manic-depressive reactions admitted to the Henry Phipps Psychiatric Clinic between 1913 and 1916. Atypical cases were not included because the author wanted to study only clear-cut, manic-depressive reactions. Several patients having what seemed to be manic excitements at the time of admission developed schizophrenic reactions on long-term observation. These cases were excluded, as were cases of depression that had lost the preponderant depressive affect and had, in the course of years, evolved slowly into more automatic and schizophrenic-like behavior. Also excluded were depressive patients with hypochondriasis who had lost most of their depressive affect and who had sunk into a state of chronic invalidism with little depressive content. The material, consequently, can be regarded as following reasonably stringent criteria for diagnosing the manic-depressive syndrome.

Follow-up on these patients was obtained by letter, by social service interview, by physician's interview, by newspaper notices of suicide, and by records from other hospitals. In only one case was no follow-up data obtained. The follow-up period evidently ranged from 35 to 39 years.

In Rennie's study, the following clinical groups were described in order of frequency: (*1*) recurrent depression: 102 patients—15 had symptom-free intervals of at least 20 years between attacks, and 52 had remissions of at least 10 years; (*2*) Cyclothymic (biphasic), 49 patients in whom all combinations were observed, with elation and depression sometimes following each other in closed cycles; (*3*) single attacks of depression, recovered—26 patients; (*4*) single attacks of depression, unrecovered—14 patients, of whom nine committed suicide; (*5*) recurrent manic attacks, 14 cases; (*6*) single manic attacks—two patients. (These remained well for over 20 years after the attack. A third patient became manic for the first time at age 40 and was still hospitalized at age 64.)

Lundquist (1945) made a longitudinal study of 319 manic-depressive patients whose first hospitalization for this disorder was at the Langbrö Hospital in the years 1912–1931. The investigator reviewed the records and checked the appropriateness of the diagnoses to "satisfy all reasonable demands in regard to reliability." His sample consisted of 123 men (38 per cent) and 196 women (62 per cent).

After locating the discharged patients, follow-up was conducted by a personal examination of the patient at the hospital, by a home visit by a social worker if the patient lived in Stockholm, by a detailed questionnaire mailed to the patient living outside of Stockholm, and by a review of the hospital record of the patient currently hospitalized elsewhere.

The period of observation varied considerably: between 20–30 years, 42 per cent; 10–20 years, 38 per cent; and less than 10 years, 20 per cent.

The duration of an episode was defined as the time that elapsed between the patient's recognition of his symptoms and his return to his former occupation. Recovery was based on the rough gauge of the patient's ability to resume his work and his ordinary mode of life.

ONSET OF EPISODES

The relative frequency of an insidious onset, as compared with an acute onset, was studied by Hopkinson (1963). One hundred consecutive inpatients diagnosed as having an affective illness were investigated. All were more than 50 years of age on admission, and 39 had suffered previous attacks before the age of 50. Eighty patients were examined personally by the author, and in the remaining 20 cases, the pertinent data were abstracted from the case histories.

When the onset of the illness was studied, it was found that 26 per cent of the cases exhibited a well-defined prodromal period; the remaining 74 per cent of the cases were considered of acute onset. Complaints made by these patients in the prodromal period were vague and nonspecific. Tension and anxiety occurred in all to some extent. The duration of the prodromal period before the onset of a clear-cut depressive psychosis ranged from 8 months to 10 years; the mean duration was 33.5 months.

In a later study (1964), Hopkinson investigated the prodromal phase in 43 younger patients (ages 16–48). Thirteen (30.2 per cent) showed a prodromal phase of 2 months to 7 years (mean = 23 months. The clinical features of the prodromal period were chiefly tension, anxiety, and indecision.

In summary, 70–75 per cent of the patients, in both studies, with an affective disorder had an acute onset.

The relationship of acuteness of onset to prognosis has been studied by several investigators. Steen (1933) found, in a study of 493 patients, that the recovery rate was higher among manic depressives who showed an acute onset than among those with a protracted onset. On the other hand, Strecker *et al.* (1931), in a comparison of 50 recovered manic depressives and 50 nonrecovered, found that an acute onset occurred no more frequently in the recovered group than in the chronic group. More recently, in a study of 96 cases grossly diagnosed as manic depressive, Astrup, Fossum, and Holmboe (1959) found that an acute onset favored recovery.

Hopkinson (1965) found a significantly higher *frequency* of attacks per patient among his cases with an acute onset (mean = 2.8) than among those patients with a prodromal phase (mean = 1.3).

Lundquist (1945) reported that patients over 30 with an acute onset (less than a month) had a significantly shorter *duration* of their episodes than those with a gradual onset. In the age group of 30–39 years, the mean duration of the acute onset cases was 5.1 months and of the gradual onset cases, 27.2 months.

The average age of onset of depression varies so widely from study to study that no definite conclusions can be made. The following statistics for the decade of peak incidence may serve as a rough guide: 20–30, Kraepelin (1913); 30–39, Stenstedt (1952), Cassidy, Flanagan, and Spellman (1957), and Ayd (1961); 45–55, Rennie (1942); and 50 and older, Lundquist (1945).

RECOVERY AND CHRONICITY

There is considerable variation among the authors on the proportion of patients remaining chronically ill following the onset of depressive illness. It is difficult to make comparisons among the various studies because different diagnostic criteria are used, the definition of chronicity varies, the periods of observation vary, and in many studies, no distinction is made between those who became chronic after the first attack and those who became chronic only after multiple attacks.

The relatively well-designed, retrospective study by Rennie indicated that approximately 3 per cent were found on long-term follow-up to be chronically ill. Kraepelin reported that 5 per cent of his cases became chronic. Lundquist reported that 79.6 per cent of the depressives recovered completely from the first attack. Age of onset was a factor: The recovery rate ranged from 92 per cent for patients less than 30 years old to 75 per cent in the 30–40 age group. It is probable that his percentages are lower than those of the others because of his more stringent definition of complete recovery.

Astrup, Fossum, and Holmboe (1959) divided their group of manic-depressive patients into the categories of "chronic," "improved," and "recovered." Of the 70 "pure" manic depressives, six (8.6 per cent) were still chronically ill at the time of follow-up. The majority had recovered completely, and a minority showed residual "instability" and were classified as improved.* The follow-up period was five years or more.

It is noteworthy that a patient may have an initial manic or depressive episode from which he recovers completely and, after a long symptom-free

---

* The precise figures for the improved and recovered categories are not available from Astrup's monograph because of the lumping together of the manic-depressive and schizoaffective patients.

interval, he may relapse into a chronic state. Rennie reports the case of a patient who had an initial episode of mania followed by depression, the entire cycle lasting about a year. He was symptom-free for 23 years afterward and then he lapsed into a state of manic excitement lasting 22 years.

Kraepelin (1913) indicates that a patient may have chronic depression of many years' duration and still have a complete remission. He presents an illustrative case (p. 143) with a single attack lasting 15 years, from which the patient made a complete recovery.

Duration

Some idea of the average or expected duration of an episode of depression is obviously important so that the physician can adequately prepare the patient and family psychologically and give them a basis for making decisions about the business affairs of the patient as well as appropriate financial arrangements for his care.

One aspect of the usual depressive episode that is of importance in treatment is the fact that the episode tends to follow a curve, i.e., tends to progressively worsen, then bottoms out, and then progressively improves until the patient returns to his premorbid state. By determining the time of onset of the depression, the physician can make a rough estimate as to when an upward turn in the cycle may be expected. It is particularly important when assessing the efficacy of specific forms of treatment to take into account the spontaneous start of the upward swing.

There is some variation in the findings of the numerous studies relevant to duration. Undoubtedly, these variations may be attributed to different methods of observation and to different criteria for making diagnoses and judging improvement. In general, the relatively unrefined clinical studies (which will be discussed presently) indicate a longer duration than do the systematic studies.

Lundquist (1945) found that the median duration of the attack of depression in patients younger than 30 was 6.3 months, and for those older than 30, 8.7 months. This difference was statistically significant. There was no significant difference between men and women in regard to duration. (As noted previously, he also found acute onset associated with shorter duration.) Paskind (1930b) also found in his outpatient group a shorter duration of attacks occurring before age 30 than after age 30. Rennie's study yielded similar results, the first episode lasting on the average 6.5 months. He found, incidentally, that the average duration of hospitalization was 2.5 months. In Paskind's series of non-hospitalized depressives, the median duration was 3 months. He found that 14 per cent of the episodes lasted one month or less, and that almost 80 per cent were completed in 6 months or less.

The earlier, less refined studies predominantly report a period of 6–18 months as the average duration of the first attack: Kraepelin (1913), 6–8 months; Pollack (1931), 1.1 years; Strecker *et al.* (1931), 1.5 years. The clinical impression of the recent writers of monographs on depression shows similar variation. Kraines (1957) states that the average depressive episode lasts about 18 months. Ayd (1961) reports that prior to age 30, the attacks average 6–12 months; between the ages of 30 and 50, they average 9–18 months; and after 50, they tend to persist longer, with many patients remaining ill from three to five years.

In regard to the *duration of multiple episodes* of depression, there has been a prevalent opinion among clinicians that there is a trend towards prolongation of the episodes with each recurrence (Kraepelin, 1913). Lundquist, however, performed a statistical analysis of the duration of multiple episodes and found there was no significant increase in duration with successive attacks. Paskind's (1930b) study of outpatient cases similarly showed that the attacks do not become longer as the disease recurs. The median duration for first attacks was four months, and for second, third, or subsequent attacks three months.

The differences in the findings between the rough clinical studies and the statistical studies may reflect a difference in samples and/or different criteria for recovery from the depression. It is probable that certain biases influenced the selection of cases in the less refined studies and, therefore, the samples cannot be considered representative.

Lundquist found a significant association between prolonged duration and the presence of delusions in younger but not older patients. The presence of confusion, on the other hand, favored a shorter duration.

Brief Attacks of Manic-Depressive Psychosis

Paskind (1929) described 88 cases of depression of very brief duration; viz., from a few hours to a few days. These patients had essentially the same symptoms as those in his other extramural cases of longer duration and constituted 13.9 per cent of his large series of cases diagnosed as manic-depressive disorder. The case histories he presents leave little doubt that they would currently be diagnosed as neurotic-depressive reaction.

Most of these patients with brief attacks also experienced longer episodes of depression. In 51, the brief attacks came first, and were followed from months to decades later by longer attacks lasting from several weeks to several years. In 18, longer attacks occurred first, and were followed by the transient episodes. In nine, there were brief episodes only.

RECURRENCE

There is considerable variation in the literature relevant to the frequency of relapses among depressed patients. Except as indicated, the

Table 3–1.
FREQUENCY OF SINGLE AND MULTIPLE ATTACKS OF DEPRESSION

Frequency of depression	Rennie		Lundquist	
	No. of patients	(%)	No. of patients	(%)
1 attack	26	21.0	105	61.0
2 attacks	33	27.0	45	26.0
3 attacks	28	23.0	11	6.5
4+attacks	36	29.0	11	6.5
TOTAL	123	100	172	100

statistics for manic-depressive psychosis include some manic patients in addition to the depressed patients. In the earlier studies, German authors reported a substantially higher incidence of recurrence than American investigators (Lundquist, 1945). These differences may be attributed to more stringent diagnostic criteria and to longer periods of observation by the German authors.

Of the more refined studies, Rennie's reported relapse rate is closer to that of the German writers than to the other American investigators. He found that 97 of 123 patients (79 per cent) initially admitted to the hospital in a depressed state subsequently had a recurrence of depression. (These figures do not include 14 patients who committed suicide after the first admission or who remained chronically ill.) When the cyclothymic cases (i.e., patients who had at least one manic attack in addition to the depression) are added to this group, the proportion of relapse is 142 patients of 170 (84 per cent).

The Scandinavian investigators Lundquist (1945) and Stenstedt (1952) reported, respectively, a 49 per cent and a 47 per cent incidence of relapse. In comparing their studies with Rennie's, one can reasonably conclude that the more stringent diagnostic criteria employed by Rennie and the longer period of observation of his sample may account for the higher percentage of relapses in his report.

The differences in relapse rate are reflected in a striking difference in the rate of multiple recurrences. In Rennie's series more than half of the depressed patients had three or more recurrences (see Table 3–1).

The frequency of multiple recurrences in the cyclothymic cases was particularly high in Rennie's series. Thirty-seven of the 47 patients in the group had four or more episodes. In Kraepelin's series, 204 out of 310 cases of this type (67 per cent) had one or more recurrences, with more than half having three or more attacks.

Another important aspect of the recurrent attacks is their duration. The opinion has frequently been expressed that the episodes become progressively longer with each recurrence. Rennie, however, in analyzing his data, found that the second episode had the same duration as the initial episode in 20 per cent, was longer in 35 per cent, and was shorter in 45 per cent. Paskind found that the median duration decreased with successive attacks.

INTERVALS BETWEEN ATTACKS

In examining the literature on the intervals between episodes of depression, one is struck by the fact that recurrences may occur after years, or even decades, of apparent good health. The systematic studies offer little encouragement for the notion of a permanent cure analogous to five-year cures reported for cancer treatment. Recurrences have been reported as long as 40 years after recovery from an initial depression (Kraepelin).

The findings presented by Rennie, in particular, are noteworthy in that the highest proportion of relapses occurred 10–20 years after the initial episode of depression. His follow-up showed the following relapse rate for his 97 cases of recurrent depressions: Recurrence less than 10 years after the first attack of depression in 35 per cent; 10–20 years, 52 per cent; more than 20 years, 13 per cent. It should be emphasized that 65 per cent had recurrences after remissions of 10–30 years.

In an earlier study, Kraepelin had tabulated the symptom-free intervals between 70 episodes of depression. Unlike Rennie's study, Kraepelin's included intervals after the second and later attacks (as well as intervals between the first and second episodes). He found that with each successive attack the intervals tended to become shorter. Since his series consisted of hospitalized patients, it is interesting to note the same trend among the extramural patients in Paskind's study. A comparison of the distribution of intervals in ten-year categories is shown in Table 3–2. For the purposes of comparison, Rennie's results are also included. It should be emphasized that his findings apply only to the *first* interval. The tendency for his

Table 3–2.

COMPARISON OF DISTRIBUTION OF TIME INTERVALS BETWEEN
MANIC-DEPRESSIVE EPISODES IN INPATIENTS AND OUTPATIENTS

Source	No. of intervals	Duration of time intervals (%)				
		0–9 yrs.	10–19 yrs.	20–29 yrs.	30–39 yrs.	More than 40 yrs.
Kraepelin (1913) (inpatients)	703	80.5	13.5	4.8	1.1	.14
Paskind (1930b) (outpatients)	438	64.0	27.8	5.7	1.6	.92
Rennie (1942) (inpatients)	97*	35.0	52.0	15.0		

* Includes only *first* interval (i.e. between first and second episodes).

Table 3–3.

COMPARISON OF MEDIAN INTERVALS FOR INPATIENTS AND OUTPATIENTS

	No. of cases	First interval (yrs.)	Second interval (yrs.)	Third and subsequent intervals (yrs.)
Inpatients (Kraepelin 1913)	167	6	2.8	2
Outpatients (Paskind 1930b)	248	8	5	4

intervals to be longer than Kraepelin's and Paskind's may be explained by the fact that the later intervals included in their study are shorter than the first intervals.

Kraepelin and Paskind show a somewhat similar distribution of the intervals, with Paskind's outpatient cases having longer periods of remission than Kraepelin's hospitalized cases.

Another way of expressing the duration of the intervals is in terms of the median duration of the specific intervals. Table 3–3 shows that the median interval is longer in the outpatient cases of Paskind, and also that in both outpatient and hospitalized cases the median intervals tend to be shorter with successive attacks.

In Kraepelin's study, the biphasic cases showed consistently shorter symptom-free intervals than the simple depressions.

Further support for the observation that after the first recurrence the interval tends to become shorter is found in Lundquist's study. In the age group older than 30, the mean duration of the first interval was about seven years, and the second interval three years. This difference was statistically significant.

Lundquist's data, classified according to three-year intervals, showed that the overwhelming preponderance of relapses occurred in the first nine years. It should be pointed out that his follow-up period was as short as 10 years in some cases, as compared to 25–30 years in Rennie's series. Hence, it is probable that many of the cases in Lundquist's series would have shown a relapse if they had been followed for a longer period than 10 years. Lundquist computed the *probability* of a relapse after a patient has recovered from an initial episode of depression (Table 3–4). These findings were tabulated separately for the young depressives and older depressives, but no significant difference was found between the two groups. It may be noted that the highest probability of recurrence was in the 3–6-year interval.

SCHIZOPHRENIC OUTCOME

In Rennie's sample of 208 cases of manic-depressive psychosis, four cases changed their character sufficiently to justify the conclusion of an

Table 3–4.

PROBABILITY OF RECURRENCE AFTER RECOVERY FROM FIRST ATTACK*

	Years after first depression				
Age at first attack	3	6	9	12	15
Age<30 years	12%	13%	4%	—	—
Age 30+years	10%	12%	9%	8%	6%

* From Lundquist (1945).

ultimate schizophrenic development. A review of these cases suggested that there was a strong component of schizophrenic symptomatology at the time of the diagnosis of manic-depressive psychosis.

Hoch and Rachlin (1941) reviewed the records of 5,799 cases of schizophrenia admitted to the Manhattan State Hospital, New York City. They found 7.1 per cent of these patients had been diagnosed as manic depressive during previous admissions. Whether there was an alteration in the nature of the disorder, an initial misclassification, or a change in diagnostic criteria, was not established by these writers.

Lewis and Piotrowski (1954) found that 38 (54 per cent) of 70 patients, originally diagnosed as manic depressives, had their diagnoses changed to schizophrenia in a 3–20-year follow-up. In reviewing the original records, the authors demonstrated that the patients whose diagnoses were changed were misclassified initially, i.e., they showed clear-cut schizophrenic signs at the time of their first admission. Because of the very loose criteria used in diagnosing manic-depressive disorder in the early decades of this century, it is difficult to determine what proportion, if any, of the clear-cut manic depressives had a schizophrenic outcome.

Lundquist reported that about 7 per cent of his manic-depressive cases eventually developed a schizophrenic picture.

Astrup, Fossum, and Holmboe (1959) isolated 70 cases of "pure" manic-depressive disorder and followed these from 7–19 years after the onset of the disorder. They found that none had a schizophrenic outcome. In contrast, 13 (50 per cent) of a group of 26 cases diagnosed as schizo-affective psychosis showed schizophrenic symptomatology on follow-up.

SUICIDE

At the present time, the only important cause of death in depression is suicide.* Previously, inanition due to lack of food and secondary infection were occasional causes of death but with modern hospital treatment such complications are unusual.

* In this section, the discussion will deal primarily with studies of suicide among depressed patients. The topic of suicide is broad and many excellent monographs are available (for example, Farberow and Schneidman, 1961; Meerloo, 1962).

The actual suicide risk among depressed patients is difficult to assess because of the incomplete follow-ups and difficulties in establishing the cause of death. Long-term follow-ups by Rennie (1942) and by Lundquist (1945) indicated that approximately 5 per cent of the patients initially diagnosed in a hospital as manic depressive (or as having one of the other depressive disorders) subsequently committed suicide. Since the national rate is about .01 per cent (Vital Statistics of the United States, 1960), their findings suggest that the risk of suicide in a patient hospitalized at some time in his life for depression is about 500 times the national average. The more recent studies, however, show a lower suicidal rate among depressed patients.

Pokorny (1964) investigated the suicide rate among former patients in a psychiatric service of a Texas veterans' hospital over a 15-year period. Using a complex actuarial system, he calculated the suicide rates per 100,000 per year as follows: depression, 566; schizophrenia, 167; neurosis, 119; personality disorder, 130; alcoholism, 133; and organic, 78. He then calculated the age-adjusted suicide rate for male Texas veterans as 22.7 per 100,000. The suicide rate for depressed patients, therefore, was 25 times the expected rate and substantially higher than that of other psychiatric patients.

Temoche, Pugh, and MacMahon (1964), studying the suicide rates among current and former mental institution patients in Massachusetts, found a substantially higher rate of suicide among depressed patients than nondepressed patients. The computed ratio for depressives was 36 times as high as for the general population and about three times as high as for either schizophrenics or alcoholics.

The suicide rate among patients who are known to be suicidal risks is apparently high. Moss and Hamilton (1956) conducted a follow-up study for periods of two months to 20 years of 50 patients who had been considered "seriously suicidal" during their previous hospitalization (average 4 years). Eleven (22 per cent) of the 50 later committed suicide. In a retrospective study of 134 suicides, Robins *et al.* (1959) found that 68 per cent had previously communicated suicidal ideas and that 41 per cent had specifically stated they intended to commit suicide.

The available figures clearly indicate that the suicidal risk is greatest during weekend leaves from the hospital and shortly after discharge from the hospital. Wheat (1960), surveying suicides among psychiatric hospital patients, found that 30 per cent committed suicide during the period of hospitalization. Sixty-three per cent of the suicides among the discharged patients occurred within one month after discharge. Temoche, Pugh, and MacMahon (1964) calculated that the suicidal risk in the first six months after discharge is 34 times greater than in the general population and in the second six months about nine times greater. About half of the suicides occurred within 11 months of release.

Many studies have reported the observation that women depressives attempt suicide more frequently than men but that men are more often successful. Kraines (1957) reported that, in his series of manic-depressive patients, twice as many women as men attempted suicide and three times as many men as women were successful suicides.

Although no data are available regarding the suicidal methods employed by depressives, the statistics for the general population may be relevant. In 1961 (Statistical Abstract of the United States, 1963), the most common method employed by men was firearms, followed by poisoning, and hanging. Poisoning was most frequently used by women (44 per cent of the women used this method as compared with 18 per cent of the men). Barbiturate overdosage accounts for 6 per cent of all suicides and 18 per cent of all accidental deaths (*Medical Tribune*, August 1962, p. 24); it is probable that many of these "accidental" deaths are unreported suicides.

There is evidence that the number of suicides each year is greater than the official report of 19,450 in the United States in 1960. Many accidental deaths actually represent concealed suicides. MacDonald (1964), for instance, collected 37 cases of attempted suicide by automobile. Some writers believe that the actual rate of suicide is three or four times as great as the official rate. The number of attempted suicides is believed to be seven or eight times the number of successful suicides (Stengel, 1962).

Homicide may occur in association with suicide among depressed patients (Campbell, 1953). Reports, for example, of a mother killing her children and then herself are not rare. One woman, who was convinced by her psychotherapist that her children needed her even though she believed herself worthless, decided to kill them as well as herself to "spare them the agony of growing up without a mother." She subsequently followed through with her plan.

The best indication of a suicidal risk is the communication of suicidal intent (Robins *et al.,* 1959). As Stengel (1962) points out, the notion that the person who talks about suicide will never carry it out is fallacious. Also, a previous unsuccessful suicidal attempt greatly increases the probability of a subsequent successful suicidal attempt (Motto, 1965).

In addition to trying to elicit suicidal wishes from the depressed patient, the clinician should look for signs of hopelessness. In our studies we found that suicidal wishes had a higher correlation with hopelessness than with any other symptom of depression. Futhermore, Pichot and Lempérière (1964), in a factor analysis of the Depression Inventory, extracted a factor containing only two variables, pessimism (hopelessness) and suicidal wishes.

CONCLUSIONS

1. Complete recovery from an episode of depression occurs in 70–95 per cent of the cases. About 95 per cent of the younger patients recover completely.

2. The median duration of the attacks is approximately 6.3 months among inpatients and approximately 3 months among outpatients. The more severe cases (i.e., those requiring hospitalization), therefore, have a longer duration than the milder cases.

3. When the initial attack occurs before age 30, it tends to be shorter than when it occurs after 30. Acute onset also favors shorter duration.

4. Contrary to prevalent opinion, there is *not* a trend towards prolongation of the attacks with each recurrence, the later attacks lasting about as long as the earlier attacks.

5. After an initial attack of depression, 47–79 per cent of the patients will have a recurrence at some time in their lives. The correct figure is probably closer to 79 per cent, because this is based on a longer follow-up period.

6. The likelihood of frequent recurrences is greater in the biphasic cases than in cases of depression without a manic phase.

7. After the first attack of depression, most patients have a symptom-free interval of more than three years before the next attack.

8. Although the duration of multiple episodes remains about the same, the symptom-free interval tends to decrease with each successive attack. In the biphasic cases the intervals are consistently shorter than in the simple depressions.

9. Whether any of the cases of pure depression have a schizophrenic outcome cannot be determined as yet, because of the relatively high percentage of incorrect diagnoses at the time of the initial episode. At most, only 5 per cent become schizophrenic after repeated attacks.

10. Approximately 5 per cent of hospitalized manic-depressive patients subsequently commit suicide. The suicidal risk is especially high on weekend leaves from the hospital and during the month following hospitalization and remains high for six months after discharge.

11. The notion that a person who threatens suicide will not carry out the threat is fallacious. The communication of suicidal intent is the best single predictor of a successful suidical attempt. Previously unsuccessful suicidal attempts are followed by successful suicides in a substantial proportion of the cases.

Chapter 4.
Classification of the
Affective Disorders

THE OFFICIAL NOMENCLATURE

To find the various types of depression in the nomenclature of the American Psychiatric Association (APA), it is necessary to hunt through many sections. This scattering of the affective disorders contrasts with the consolidation found in other classification systems [e.g., the British Classification (Fleming, 1933)]. It is a reflection of several historical trends, including the dissolution of Kraepelin's grand union of all affective disorders into the manic-depressive category, the isolation of new entities such as neurotic-depressive reaction, and the attempt to separate the disorders on the basis of presumed etiological differences.

In the major division of "psychotic disorders" in the APA nomenclature, the heading "Disorders due to disturbance of metabolism, growth, nutrition, or endocrine function" embraces a single category, *involutional psychotic reaction*. This etiological heading is misleading because it suggests an organic basis for involutional depressions, although there is no more evidence of organicity in this form of depression than in any other. There is no provision, moreover, for the coding of the two types, melancholic and paranoid, found in the previous edition of the nomenclature (Cheney, 1934). This change may have unfortunate consequences, since it fuses two syndromes of later life that may be etiologically, as well as phenomenologically, distinct.

Under the title, "Disorders of psychogenic origin or without clearly defined tangible cause or structural change" we find the *manic-depressive reaction* and the new category, *psychotic depressive reaction*. The inclusion of these depressive reactions under this etiological title is questionable, since there is no more evidence of psychogenicity in these disorders than in any other affective disorder.

The *schizo-affective disorder*, which has salient affective features, is currently listed as a subtype of the schizophrenic reaction. The appropriateness of this placement is also open to question. In terms of its historical conceptualization, its course, and its prognosis, this disorder may be more closely allied to manic-depressive reaction.

The *depressive reaction,* the current form of the reactive depression, previously considered an offshoot of manic-depressive psychosis (Cheney, 1934), gains complete autonomy under the "psychoneurotic reactions."

DERIVATION OF SYSTEM OF CLASSIFICATION

The present system of classification represents a composite of the ideas of three schools of thought: those of Emil Kraepelin, Adolph Meyer, and Sigmund Freud. The division of the various nosological categories, particularly of the psychoses, reflects the original boundaries drawn by Kraepelin. The major modification in the terminology reflects the Meyerian influence. Meyer rejected the Kraepelinian concept of disease entities, and formulated in its place a theory of "reaction types." The reaction types were conceived by him to be the result of the interaction between the specific hereditary endowment and the matrix of psychological and social forces impinging on the organism. The term reaction in the nomenclature reflects the Meyerian view.

Freud's influence is seen in the descriptions of the specific categories in the glossary section of the APA Manual. Here the syndromes are outlined according to the psychoanalytic theories; the various affective disorders are presented in terms of the concepts of guilt, retroflected hostility, and defense against anxiety.

RELIABILITY AND VALIDITY OF CLASSIFICATION

Many recent studies in the United States and the United Kingdom have cast doubt on the reliability of the official nomenclatures. Some investigators, however, suggest that the essential problem may be in the *application* of the nomenclature, rather than in its construction (Kreitman *et al.,* 1961; Beck *et al.,* 1962; Ward *et al.,* 1962). In our studies, for instance, we found that there were substantial discrepancies among diagnosticians concurrently interviewing the same patients. We also found, however, that we could improve diagnostic agreement considerably by formulating operational definitions of the categories in the official nomenclature.

The validity of a nomenclature refers to the accuracy with which the diagnostic terms designate veridical entities. Unfortunately, in the case of the so-called functional psychiatric disorders, there has been no known pathology or physiological abnormality to provide guidelines in the construction of the nomenclature. The basic definition of the nosological categories has rested entirely on clinical criteria.

In assessing the validity of a medical or psychiatric classification, it is appropriate to ask whether the specific groups or syndromes isolated from each other are different in ways that are of medical or psychiatric significance, that is, in terms of symptoms, duration, outcome, tendency to recur, and response to treatment. In general, the studies made seem to justify the isolation of the group of depressive disorders from other psychiatric disorders; in addition, there is some support for the separation within the affective group of the *endogenous* depressions from the *reactive* depressions.

Clark and Mallet (1963) conducted a follow-up study of cases of depression and schizophrenia in young adults. Seventy-four cases were diagnosed as manic-depressive psychosis or reactive depression and 76 patients who were initially diagnosed as schizophrenics were followed for three years. During the follow-up period, 70 per cent of the schizophrenics were readmitted, as were 20 per cent of the depressives. Thirteen (17 per cent) of the schizophrenics became chronic, as compared with only 1 (1.3 per cent) of the depressives. Of the 15 depressed patients requiring readmission to the hospital, four were considered to have schizophrenia at that time. Of the 76 patients initially diagnosed as schizophrenic, none was considered to have a depressive disorder on readmission.

Treatment responses have recently been correlated with the major diagnostic categories. It has been found that patients diagnosed as schizophrenic tend to respond favorably to the administration of phenothiazines, whereas patients who are primarily depressed tend to improve with either electroconvulsive treatment (ECT) or the so-called antidepressant drugs.

Several inferences may be drawn from the clinical studies. Two major categories are distinguishable (as Kraepelin suggested) when rate of recovery and chronicity are examined as parts of the clinical picture. These are (1) depressive disorders having a relatively high rate of complete recovery, a low rate of relapse within three years of the initial diagnosis, and a low rate of chronicity; and (2) schizophrenia having a high rate of relapse and a high rate of chronicity. Some cases that initially evince the clinical picture of depression ultimately develop symptoms of schizophrenia. But it is rare for a patient who has symptoms of schizophrenia to develop manic-depressive symptoms later. Lewis and Piotrowski (1954) suggest that many cases are diagnosed incorrectly as manic depressives because of insufficient recognition of certain signs of schizophrenia. The major division between these two disorders is further upheld by the differential effectiveness of certain treatments.

There is much less evidence in support of the subcategories within the group of affective disorders. Considerable doubt remains regarding the validity of dividing Kraepelin's aggregate category, manic-depressive psychosis, into involutional psychotic reaction, neurotic-depressive reaction, and psychotic depressive reaction. If these subcategories can be justified, then provision must be made in the nomenclature for classifying mild manic states, such as a "hypomanic reaction," which would be analogous to neurotic-depressive reaction.

DICHOTOMIES AND DUALISMS

Many authorities such as Aubrey Lewis (1938) and Paul Hoch (1953) regard depression as essentially a single entity, while others slice the syndrome along various planes to produce several dichotomies. This controversy reflects fundamental differences between the unitary and the separatist schools (Partridge, 1949). The unitary school (gradualists) maintains that depression is a single clinical disorder that can express itself in a variety of forms; the separatists state that there are several distinguishable types.

Endogenous vs. Exogenous

This division attempts to establish the basic etiology of depression. Cases of depression are divided into those caused essentially by internal factors (endogenous), and those caused by external factors (exogenous). Although originally the exogenous group included such environmental agents as toxins and bacteria, recent writers have equated exogenous with psychogenic factors. This dichotomy will be discussed at greater length below.

Autonomous vs. Reactive

Some writers have made a distinction between types of depression on the basis of their degree of reactivity to external events. Gillespie (1929) described several groups of depressed patients that differed in their responsiveness to external influences. He labelled those cases that followed a relentless course irresponsive of any favorable environmental influences as "autonomous." Those that responded favorably to encouragement and understanding were labelled "reactive."

Agitated vs. Retarded

Depression has often been characterized in terms of the predominant activity level. Many authors consider agitation as characteristic of depressions of the involutional period and retardation as characteristic of earlier depressions. Recent studies have discounted this hypothesis.

Psychotic vs. Neurotic

Most contemporary authors draw a sharp line between psychotic and neurotic depressions. The gradualists, however (Lewis, 1938; Hoch; 1953), believe that this distinction is artificial, and that the differences are primarily quantitative. They assert that the reported distinctions are based entirely on differences in the severity of the illness.

ENDOGENOUS AND EXOGENOUS DEPRESSIONS

The focus of the controversy between the separatists and the gradualists has been primarily on the etiological concepts of depression. The separatists favor two distinct entities. One category consists of cases that are *endogenous,* i.e., caused primarily by some biological derangement in the human organism. The second category, viz., *reactive depressions,* consists of cases caused primarily by some external stress (bereavement, financial reverses, loss of employment). The former includes manic-depressive psychosis and involutional melancholia; the latter consists of reactive, psychogenic, or neurotic, depression. The unitary school considers these distinctions artificial and does not recognize the validity of labelling some cases endogenous and others reactive.

The concept of two etiologically different types of depression is not new. In 1586 Timothy Bright, a physician, wrote a monograph, *Melancholy and the Conscience of Sinne,* in which he distinguished two different types of depression. He described one type "where the perill is not of the body" and requires "cure of the minde" (i.e., psychotherapy). In the second type, "the melancholy humour, deluding the organical actions, abuseth the minde;" this type requires physical treatment.

ORIGIN OF ENDOGENOUS-EXOGENOUS MODEL

The words "endogen" and "exogen" were coined by the Swiss botanist Augustin de Candolle (1816). The concept was introduced into psychiatry toward the end of the nineteenth century by the German neuropsychiatrist P. J. Moebius.* Moebius attached the label of "endogenous" to the group of mental disorders considered at that time to be due to degeneration or hereditary factors (internal causes). He further distinguished another group of mental disorders that he considered to be produced by bacterial, chemical, and other toxins (external causes); this group was given the label of "exogenous." The endogenous-exogenous view of psychiatric disorders was a completely organic dichotomy that left no room for a different order of causative agents, namely the social or psychogenic. The exclusiveness of this doctrine caused semantic difficulties when the concept later had to be adapted to include social determinants of abnormal behavior.

The dualism inherent in the endogenous-exogenous concept is apparent in the writing of Kraepelin (1913). He accepted Moebius's classification and stated that the principal demarcation of etiology of mental disorders is between *internal* and *external* causes. He proposed that there was a natural division between the two major groups of diseases, exogenous and endogenous: In manic-depressive illness, "the real causes of the malady must be

---

* For a more complete discussion of the evolution of the concept, see Heron (1965).

sought in permanent internal changes which very often, perhaps always, are innate." Environment could at most be a precipitant of manic-depressive disease, because by definition an endogenous illness could not at the same time be an exogenous illness.

"THE GREAT DEBATES"

The controversy regarding the endogenous-exogenous concept has been most prominent in Great Britain, and a number of outstanding authorities have taken part on both sides of the argument (Partridge, 1949). Earlier, Kraepelin had endeavored to include almost all forms of depression under one label, manic-depressive disorder. Later, German writers, with their tendency to formalism and categorization, almost uniformly split depressions into endogenous and exogenous. The British, however, have been sharply divided on this point, and as a result of the clash of opinions in a series of great debates, the concepts of depression have been considerably refined (although unanimity has not as yet been attained).

The first of the debates was touched off by Mapother in 1926, when he attacked the notion of a clinical distinction between neurotic depressions and psychotic depressions. (This argument later shaded into the controversy of endogenous versus reactive depression.) He held that the only reason for making a distinction was the practical difficulties connected with commitment procedures. He claimed that he could "find no other basis for the distinction; neither insight, nor cooperation in treatment, nor susceptibility to psychotherapy." He attacked the notion that there are neurotic conditions that are purely psychogenic and psychotic conditions that are dependent on structural change. His view was that all depressions, whether ostensibly psychogenic or seemingly endogenous, are mediated by essentially the same means.

Mapother's concept is an interesting statement of the phenomenon of depression: "The essence of an attack is the clinical fact that the emotions for the time have lost enduring relation to current experience and whatever their origin and intensity they have achieved a sort of autonomy." There were a number of rebuttals in the discussion of Mapother's paper, and then another debate in 1930, which touched off another series of discussions and papers (see Partridge).

DISTINCTION BETWEEN ENDOGENOUS AND REACTIVE DEPRESSIONS

From the various conflicting as well as complimentary opinions regarding the validity of differentiating endogenous from reactive or neurotic depressions, it is possible to make a composite picture of endogenous depression as it emerged from the debates. This may be helpful in understanding the referents of the term endogenous, which is widely used in the literature, although it is not included in any official nomenclature.

In general, there are two major defining characteristics of the category *endogenous depression*. First, it is generally equated with psychosis and is consequently distinguished from neurotic depressions. Second, it is regarded as arising primarily from internal (physiological) factors and can thus be contrasted with reactive depressions produced by external stress. To complicate the distinctions, however, reactive depressions, although often equated with neurotic depressions, are sometimes distinguished from them.

The *etiology* of endogenous depression has been ascribed to a toxic chemical agent, to a hormonal factor, or to a metabolic disturbance (Crichton-Miller, 1930; Boyle, 1930). The autonomy from external environmental stimuli was considered an essential feature. Crichton-Miller likened the mood variation to the swinging of a pendulum, completely independent of the environment. Neurotic variations in mood, in contrast, were compared to the motion of a boat with insufficient keel, subject to the oscillations in its milieu.

The specific *symptomatology* has been characterized as a diffuse coloring of the whole outlook, phasic morning-evening variation, continuity, detachment from reality, loss of affection, and loss of power to grieve (Buzzard, 1930). To this should be added Gillespie's observation that the symptoms seem alien to the individual and not congruent with his premorbid personality.

The role of *heredity* in endogenous depressions has been stressed by a number of writers. Gillespie (1929) reported that a family history of psychosis is common in this group, and Buzzard (1930) suggested that suicide and alcoholism are frequent in the family background. *Constitutional factors* as reflected in body build were emphasized by Strauss.

Reactive depressions are distinguished from endogenous depressions because they fluctuate according to ascertainable psychological factors (Gillespie, 1929). In terms of the symptomatology, the distinguishing features are a tendency to blame the environment, and insight into the abnormal nature of the condition.

DEPRESSIVE EQUIVALENTS

Many writers have attempted to spread the umbrella of depression to cover cases showing clinical symptoms or behaviors different from those generally indicative of depression. The term *depressive equivalents* was introduced by Kennedy and Wiesel (1946) to describe patients who had various somatic complaints but who did not show any apparent mood depression. They reported three cases characterized by somatic pain, sleep disturbance, and weight loss, all of whom recovered completely after a course of ECT.

A number of other terms have been applied to designate such cases of concealed depression. These include: incomplete depression, latent depression, atypical depression, and masked depression. Various psychosomatic disorders, hypochondriacal reactions, anxiety reactions, phobic reactions, and obsessive-compulsive reactions have also been implicated as masking the typical picture of depressive reactions (Kral, 1958).

The use of such a term as depressive equivalents raises many difficult conceptual, semantic, and diagnostic problems: (1) How can a syndrome substitute for a depressive reaction? (2) Since the usual indices of depression are lacking, how can the diagnosis of masked depression, etc. be made? (3) Since the concept of depressive equivalent is so loose, it could be stretched to encompass practically any psychiatric or somatic syndrome.

One of the main criteria for diagnosing a depressive equivalent has been the response of patients with formerly intractable symptoms to ECT (Kennedy and Wiesel). Denison and Yaskin (1944), in a report on "Medical and surgical masquerades of the depressed state," list several criteria for the diagnosis of an underlying depression. These include: previous attacks of somatic complaints similar to the present attack, with complete recovery after several months, disturbance of sleep cycle, loss of appetite, loss of energy disproportionate to the somatic complaints, diurnal variation in intensity of somatic symptoms, and feeling of unreality.

It is apparent that more systematic work must be done in describing the phenomenology of these states and in defining their similarities to and differences from manifest depression.

In the consideration of disguised depressions, it is worth emphasizing the truism that depression may mask organic disease as well as vice versa. This subject is discussed in detail by Sandler (1948).

DEPRESSIONS SECONDARY TO SOMATIC DISORDERS

Depressions have been observed in association with a wide variety of nonpsychiatric disorders. In some instances, the depression appears to be a manifestation of the physiological disturbance caused by structural disease or toxic agents. In other instances, the depression seems to be a psychological reaction to being acutely or chronically ill, i.e., the illness is a nonspecific precipitating factor. In either event, the depressive symptomatology *per se* is not distinguishable from that observed in primary depressions (Lewis, 1934).

Conditions that specifically impair the normal functioning of the nervous system may produce depression (Castelnuovo-Tedesco, 1961). These conditions may be acute (the acute brain syndromes) such as those associated with alcohol, drugs, head trauma, or post-ictal states. Or the conditions may be chronic (chronic brain syndromes) such as those associated with cerebral arteriosclerosis, senile dementia, neurosyphilis, multiple sclerosis, malnutrition, and various vitamin deficiency syndromes.

Depression as a complication of the use of the tranquilizing drugs has frequently been reported. Early reports of the use of reserpine in the treatment of hypertension implicated this drug as a causative agent in many depressions. More recently, the phenothiazines have been suspected. Simonson (1964), for instance, interviewed 480 patients who were having their first acknowledged depression. He found that 146 (30 per cent) had been taking a phenothiazine prior to the depression. Ayd (1958), on the other hand, is skeptical of the role of the tranquilizers in producing a depression. He studied 47 cases of so-called *drug-induced depression*, and concluded that each case presented a history of predisposition to psychic disturbance and of physical and psychological stresses which helped to precipitate the depression.

Depressive symptomatology has been found in a substantial proportion of patients hospitalized for medical disorders (Schwab *et al.*, 1965; 1966). Yaskin (1931) and Yaskin, Weisenberg, and Pleasants (1931) reported a high frequency in patients with organic disease of the abdominal organs, particularly carcinoma of the pancreas. Dovenmuehle and Verwoerdt (1962) reported that 64 per cent of 62 patients hospitalized for definitely diagnosed cardiac disease had depressive symptoms of moderate or severe degree.

Other types of generalized somatic disorders that, according to Castelnuovo-Tedesco, are likely to be complicated by depression are: (1) certain infectious diseases—especially infectious hepatitis, influenza, infectious mononucleosis, atypical pneumonia, rheumatic fever, and tuberculosis; (2) so-called psychosomatic disorders such as ulcerative colitis, asthma, neurodermatitis, and rheumatoid arthritis; (3) anemias; (4) malignancies; and (5) endocrine disturbances.

In view of the popular theory that primary depression is caused by an endocrine disturbance, it is interesting that certain diseases of the endocrine glands are associated with a high frequency of depression. Michael and Gibbons (1963) point out that the adrenocortical hyperfunction of Cushing's syndrome is almost always accompanied by mood change. The alteration in mood is generally depressive, but it may also be characterized by emotional lability and over-reactiveness. In their review of the reports of psychiatric disturbance related to Cushing's syndrome, Michael and Gibbons state that the incidence of psychiatric disturbance generally exceeds 50 per cent. Severe mental disturbance, extreme enough to warrant the label *psychotic,* is found in 15–20 per cent of the cases. In one series, 12 out of 13 patients with Cushing's syndrome were reported to be consistently or intermittently depressed. There was, however, no close correlation between the symptoms of depression and the steroid output.

Michael and Gibbons also reviewed the incidence of depression in Addison's disease. They noted that depression occurred in 25 per cent of the cases, and, somewhat surprisingly, euphoria occurred in 50 per cent. Psychiatric disturbances have also been reported in cases of hypopituitarism. In longstanding untreated cases, the symptoms may appear in an extreme form. The most prominent symptom tends to be apathy and inactivity. Mild depression, occasionally interrupted by brief episodes of irritability and quarrelsomeness, is also prominent.

Chapter 5.
Neurotic and Psychotic Depressive Reactions

There is considerable controversy among authorities regarding the separation of psychotic and neurotic depressions. Although this cleavage has been part of the official nomenclature for many years, authorities such as Paul Hoch (1953) question the distinction. Hoch states:

The dynamic manifestations, the orality, the super-ego structure, etc., are the same in both, and usually the differentiation is made arbitrarily. If the patient has had some previous depressive attacks, he would probably be placed in the psychotic group; if not, he would be placed in the neurotic one. If the patient's depression is developed as a reaction to an outside precipitating factor, then he is often judged as having a neurotic depression. If such factors are not demonstrated, he is classified then as an endogenous depression. Actually there is no difference between a so-called psychotic or a so-called neurotic depression. The difference is only a matter of degree.

Hoch's statement epitomizes the point of view of the *gradualists* as opposed to the concept of the *separatists,* who make a dichotomy between neurotic and psychotic depression. The historical precedent for the gradualist concept is found in Kraepelin's statement (1913):

"We include in the manic-depressive group certain slight and slightest colorings of mood, some of them periodic, some of them continuously morbid, which on the one hand are to be regarded as the rudiment of more severe disorders; on the other hand, passing over without sharp boundary into the domain of personal predisposition."

Paskind (1930b) also believed that the psychotic depressions are simply severe forms of the manic-depressive syndrome. They differ from the milder forms in terms of the dramatic symptoms, but not in terms of any fundamental factors. He stated (p. 789):

"The situation is somewhat similar, for example, to what descriptions of diabetes would be if only hospital cases were described. Almost every case of diabetes would then show acidosis, coma, gangrene, and massive infection."

Separating depression into two distinct disorders would, according to Paskind, be analogous to separating diabetes into two distinct entities on the basis of severity.

The preponderant opinion in the contemporary literature, however, favors the separation of the neurotic and psychotic depressions. Some support for the two-disease concept is provided by the studies of Kiloh and Garside (1963), and Carney, Roth, and Garside (1965). These authors demonstrated, through the use of factor analysis, a bipolar factor, the poles corresponding to neurotic depression and endogenous depression, respectively (see Chapter 4). Sandifer, Wilson, and Green (1966) obtained a bimodal distribution of scores on their rating scale, which they interpreted as representing two types of depression. The bimodal distribution, however, may depend on the type of instrument employed. Schwab *et al.* (1967), for instance, found a bimodal distribution of scores on the Hamilton Rating Scale but not on the Beck Depression Inventory.

PSYCHONEUROTIC DEPRESSIVE REACTION

DEFINITION

In the American Psychiatric Association diagnostic manual (1952), this syndrome is characterized as follows:

The reaction is precipitated by a current situation, frequently by some loss sustained by the patient, and is often associated with a feeling of guilt for past failures or deeds. . . . The term is synonymous with 'reactive depression' and is to be differentiated from the corresponding psychotic reaction. In this differentiation, points to be considered are (1) life history of patient, with special reference to mood swings (suggestive of psychotic reaction), to the personality structure (neurotic or cyclothymic), and to precipitating environmental factors, and (2) absence of malignant symptoms (hypochondriacal preoccupation, agitation, delusions, particularly somatic, hallucinations, severe guilt feelings, intractable insomnia, suicidal ruminations, severe psychomotor retardation, profound retardation of thought, stupor).

In addition to this statement regarding the manifest characteristics of this condition, the following psychodynamic formulation is included in the manual: "The anxiety in this reaction is allayed, and hence partially relieved, by depression and self-depreciation. . . . The degree of the reaction in such cases is dependent upon the intensity of the patient's ambivalent feeling towards his loss (love, possession) as well as upon the realistic circumstances of the loss." The value of this formulation will be discussed presently.

Although not specified in the manual, the defining characteristics of psychoneurotic-depressive reaction may be assumed to be the generally accepted features of depression. The more *malignant* symptoms indicative of a psychotic depression are mentioned above. It is noteworthy that the authors consider the presence of suicidal ruminations to exclude a diagnosis of neurotic depression. This notion is contradicted by the finding that this symptom was found in 58 per cent of patients diagnosed as neurotic-depressive reaction (Table 5–1). A patient with a low mood such as dejection, low self-esteem, indecisiveness, and, possibly, some of the physical and vegetative symptoms mentioned in Chapter 2, may be considered to have a neurotic-depressive reaction.

In addition to the brief description of the manifest symptoms, the glossary also introduces two etiologic concepts. The first, viz., that the depression is precipitated by a current situation, is a derivative of the concept of reactive depression, the development of which will be discussed. The second etiologic concept is that the depression is a defense against anxiety and that the ambivalent feelings towards the presumed lost object determine the intensity of the reaction.

This specific psychodynamic formulation represents an attempt by the authors of the manual to provide a psychological explanation for this condition. It is not clear whether the psychodynamic formulation is intended to be a defining characteristic of the category. It would seem that the attempt should be regarded as *experimental,* and the validity of the category should not depend on the validity of the psychodynamic formulation or on whether it is possible to discern this particular configuration in a given case. Reports of investigators trying to apply the psychodynamic formulation have questioned its usefulness in making the diagnosis (Ascher, 1952; Ward *et al.,* 1962). The concept that neurotic-depressive reaction is *reactive* seems to be more integral to the definition of this syndrome and it may be considered, at least by some, that if some external stress cannot be demonstrated in a particular case, then the use of this diagnosis is not justified in that case.

Despite the inclusion of this category in many nomenclatures, it is by no means generally accepted. In fact, a large number of writers on depression seem to accept the *gradualist* or *unitary concept,* viz., that the difference between neurotic and psychotic depression is one of degree, and that there is no more justification in constructing separate categories than there is for dividing scarlet fever into two groups such as mild and severe. Proponents of this point of view include the authors who have written most extensively about depression, such as Mapother (1926) and Lewis (1934) in England, and Ascher (1952), Cassidy, Flanagan, and Spellman (1957), Campbell (1953), Kraines (1957), Robins *et al.* (1959), and Winokur and Pitts (1965) in the United States.

Table 5–1.

FREQUENCY OF CLINICAL FEATURES IN NEUROTIC DEPRESSIVE REACTION (NDR)
AND PSYCHOTIC DEPRESSIVE REACTION (PDR)

Clinical feature	Feature present		Present to severe degree	
	NDR (%) (n=50)	PDR (%) (n=50)	NDR (%) (n=50)	PDR (%) (n=50)
Sad facies	86	94	4	24
Stooped posture	58	76	4	20
Speech: slow, etc.	66	70	8	22
Low mood	84	80	8	44
Diurnal variation of mood	22	48	2	10
Hopelessness	78	68	6	34
Conscious guilt	64	44	6	12
Feeling inadequate	68	70	10	42
Somatic preoccupation	58	66	6	24
Suicidal wishes	58	76	14	40
Indecisiveness	56	70	6	28
Loss of motivation	70	82	8	48
Loss of interest	64	78	10	44
Fatigability	80	74	8	48
Loss of appetite	48	76	2	40
Sleep disturbance	66	80	12	52
Constipation	28	56	2	16

n = No. of patients.

EVOLUTION OF THE CONCEPT

In order to evaluate the clinical and conceptual basis for this nosological category, it might be helpful first to trace its development. In the
gradual evolution of the concept, there have been a number of radical
twists and turns so that there is little resemblance between the term as it is
now understood and its original conception.

In the earlier classifications, the reactive-depressive category was not
fused with neurotic depression as it is today. Kraepelin recognized a condition similar to the current notion of neurotic depressions and allocated
it to the category of congenital neurasthenia which he listed under constitutional psychopathic states. He also referred to a group of "psychogenic
depressions" that he considered to differ from the manic-depressive psychosis. Patients with psychogenic depressions showed a high degree of
reactivity to external situations and their depression tended to improve
when the external situation improved. The manic-depressive attack, in
contrast, was not primarily the result of an external stress situation and,
once started, it continued independent of the precipitating circumstances
and ran its own course.

Bleuler (1924) evidently allocated the milder depressions to the manic-depressive category, as indicated by his statement that "probably everything designated as periodic neurasthenia, recurrent dyspepsia, and neurasthenic melancholias belong entirely to manic-depressive insanity." He also conceded the existence of psychogenic depressions: "Simple psychogenic depressions, occurring in psychopaths not of the manic-depressive group and reaching the intensity of a mental disease, are rare."

The most definite precursor of the concept of neurotic-depressive reaction was that of reactive depression. In 1926, Lange listed psychogenic and reactive depression separately in his classification of depression. He differentiated psychogenic depressions from the endogenous variety on the basis of greater aggressiveness, egocentricity, stubbornness, and overt hostility. In addition, he stated that there were no discernible variations in mood in the psychogenic depressions. Changes in the milieu influenced this condition, and it became better when the personality conflict was solved. Wexberg (1928) described seven different groups of "mild depressive states." He included a "reactive group," but made no distinction between neurotic and psychotic in his classification.

Paskind (1929) described 663 cases of mild manic-depressive disorder seen in outpatient practice. Harrowes (1933) defined six groups of depression which included separate categories for the reactive and psychoneurotic types. Patients classified as psychoneurotic depressives showed "psychopathy, neuropathy, anxiety attacks, feelings of failure in life, sex trauma, unreality feelings and a greater subjectively than objectively depressed mood." This condition occurred in the third decade of life and, while mild, tended toward chronicity.

Aubrey Lewis (1934), in his classic paper on depression, stated that a careful analysis of 61 cases indicated that the neurotic symptoms appeared with equal frequency among the reactive and the endogenous forms of depression. He stressed that no sharp line could be drawn between psychotic and neurotic depressions.

It is apparent that despite the objections of authorities such as Lewis, there was a dominant tendency among nosographers to separate reactive and neurotic depressions from other types of depressions. The concepts of reactive and of neurotic depressions gradually converged. The fusion of these categories occurred officially in 1934. At that time, the American Psychiatric Association approved a new classification in which reactive depression was subsumed under the psychoneuroses. This concept did not attain wide currency in the decade that followed, however, as indicated by the failure of most American textbooks and reference books on psychiatry to include a category of depression among the psychoneuroses.

The new category, reactive depression, was defined in Cheney's *Outlines for Psychiatric Examinations* (1934) as follows:

"Here are to be classified those cases which show depression in reaction to obvious external causes which might naturally produce sadness, such as bereavement, sickness, and financial and other worries. The reaction of a more marked degree and of longer duration than normal sadness, may be looked upon as pathological. The deep depression with motor and mental retardation are not present, but these reactions *may be more closely related in fact to the manic-depressive reactions than to the psychoneuroses."* [My italics]

At this stage in its development, the concept of neurotic depression was still closely allied to the all-embracing category of manic-depressive disorder.

The next step in the evolution of the current concept was a major thrust in the direction of the current etiologic concept. In the United States War Department classification, adopted in 1945, the term *neurotic depressive reaction* was used. The term *reaction* represented a clearcut deviation from the Kraepelinian notion of a defined disease entity, and incorporated Adolph Meyer's psychobiological concept of an interaction of a particular type of personality with the environment. Since the presence of a specific external stress was more salient in an army at war than in civilian practice, the emphasis on reaction to stress seemed to gain increased plausibility.

The other significant departure in the definition in the Army nomenclature was the introduction of two psychoanalytic hypotheses, viz., (1) that depression represents an attempt to allay anxiety through the mechanism of introjection, and (2) that depression is related to *repressed aggression*. It states:

"The anxiety in this reaction is allayed, and, hence, partially relieved by self-depreciation through the mental mechanism of introjection. It is often associated with guilt for past failure or deeds. . . . This reaction is a nonpsychotic response precipitated by a current situation—frequently some loss sustained by the patient—although dynamically the depression is usually related to a repressed (unconscious) aggression."

The United States War Department classification received an extensive trial in the armed forces and was subsequently adopted in a slightly revised form by the Veterans Administration. The opinion of psychiatrists using the nomenclature, both in the Army and at Veterans Administration clinics and hospitals, was evidently favorable, because this classification was subsequently used as the basis for the 1952 *Diagnostic Manual* of the American Psychiatric Association. The new categories of neurotic-depressive reaction and psychotic-depressive reaction had become firmly established.

CRITIQUE OF CONCEPT

The preponderant evidence seems to favor the usefulness and validity of the category of neurotic-depressive reaction when used as a descriptive concept. Despite Ascher's criticisms (1952), the group seems to be relatively homogeneous. The recent systematic studies by Kiloh and Garside (1962) and by Carney, Roth, and Garside (1965) provide statistical evidence that a number of clinical features distinguish the syndrome from endogenous depression. It has also been demonstrated many times that patients diagnosed as neurotic-depressive reaction tend to respond poorly to electroconvulsive therapy, but cases of psychotic or endogenous depression tend to have a favorable response.

One observation that deserves further consideration is that some patients who experience one or more typical episodes of neurotic-depressive reaction later develop psychotic-depressive reactions and/or manic reactions (Paskind, 1930b). In such cases, the early neurotic attacks seem to be mild or abortive forms of manic-depressive psychosis. In specific episodes, furthermore, a patient may initially show a typical clinical picture of neurotic depression but, as the illness progresses, will begin to show increasingly more signs of a psychotic-depressive reaction.

Case Example

The patient was a 25-year-old engineer, who gave the following spontaneous description of his problem: "I am feeling very depressed. I feel as though I'm dragging myself down as well as my family. I have caused my parents no end of aggravation. The best thing would be if I dug a hole and buried myself in it. If I would get rid of myself, everybody would be upset for a time but then they would get over it. They would be better off without me."

The immediate life situation related to his depression was a job he had taken three months before. After graduating from college, he had had a succession of jobs and had started a small business that failed. He was not doing well in his current position and was certain that he would be fired within a few days. He experienced a gradual loss of self-confidence as his work did not seem to measure up to the expectations of his employer. Two days before his psychiatic consultation he received notice that he would be fired. He became very discouraged and experienced a complete loss of appetite and considerable difficulty in sleeping. He thought of various ways of killing himself, such as taking an overdose of pills or throwing himself from a high building.

A day before his consultation with me, he called his older brother to inform him that he was leaving town. His intention at that time was to commit suicide in a distant city. His brother suspected that something was wrong, so he came over to visit and talk to him. After discussing the problem with his brother, the patient began to feel better. His brother told him he would lend him money to tide him over until he could get another position and he also made arrangements for the patient to start psychotherapy. The patient went to a football game that afternoon and began to feel better since his favorite team won.

When I saw him the following day, he looked dejected and moderately depressed. He did not show any retardation or agitation. I administered the Depression Inventory. His cumulative score of 20 indicated a moderate depression. He acknowledged having the following symptoms: continual unremitting sadness;

discouragement; feelings of being a failure; lack of satisfaction; guilt feelings for "having let everybody down"; self-dislike; self-reproach; suicidal wishes; some loss of interest in other people; indecisiveness; insomnia; anorexia; and easy fatigability.

After the initial interview, which consisted of supportive psychotherapy in addition to history taking, the patient said he felt much better. During the next two or three days he was practically symptom free, and then he had a mild recurrence of his symptoms. He was seen in psychotherapy twice more at weekly intervals, and his depression cleared up completely and did not return. During this period of time, moreover, arrangements were made for him to obtain another job that was more in keeping with his particular abilities.

There are several noteworthy features about this case that are relevant to the definition of *neurotic depression.* (1) The patient developed the depression in response to certain stressful external situations. (2) The intensity of the feeling was considerably alleviated by interpersonal factors. (3) When there was a change in the external situation, the depression cleared up completely. (4) The content of the depressed thinking revolved around the precipitating event.

PSYCHOTIC DEPRESSIVE REACTION

The term *psychotic depressive reaction* does not appear in any of the official American or European classifications prior to the end of World War II. In 1951, the standard Veterans Administration classification included this term. In 1952, it was included in the official classification of the American Psychiatric Association. In the glossary accompanying this nomenclature, psychotic-depressive reaction was characterized as including patients who are severely depressed and who give evidence of gross misinterpretation of reality, including at times delusions and hallucinations.

The nomenclature distinguishes this reaction from the manic-depressive reaction, depressed type, on the basis of the following features: absence of a history of repeated depressions or of marked psychothymic mood swing, and presence of environmental precipitating factors. This category evidently is considered to be the analogue of the neurotic-depressive reaction and a present day counterpart of the reactive psychotic depressions described in the German literature in the 1920's. There are several features relevant to this diagnostic category that have troubled some authorities in the field, many of whom do not accept the distinction between neurotic-depressive reaction and psychotic-depressive reaction. The first depressive episode of a typical manic-depressive disorder may very well appear in reaction to some environmental stress (Kraepelin, 1913). On the basis of symptomatology, there are no criteria to distinguish the psychotic-depressive reaction from the depressed phase of the manic-depressive reaction.

The characteristics of psychotic-depressive reaction are illustrated in the following cases,* selected from a group of soldiers who experienced psychotic-depressive reaction after accidentally killing their buddies during the Korean War. The cases had the following common features relevant to the concept of psychotic-depressive reaction: (1) the psychosis followed a specific event that was highly disturbing to the patient; (2) there were clear-cut psychotic symptoms such as delusions and hallucinations; (3) the content of the patients' preoccupations, delusions, and hallucinations revolved around the dead buddy; (4) the typical symptoms of depression were present—depressed mood, hopelessness, suicidal wishes, and self-recriminations; (5) the patients recovered completely after a course of ECT or psychotherapy; and (6) there was no previous history of depression or mood swings.

Case 1

A 21-year-old soldier was referred to Valley Forge Army Hospital from a disciplinary barracks to which he had been confined for "culpable negligence." While near the line in Korea, he and his best buddy, Buck, had been working very hard laying wire. They paused to take a break and started "fooling around" and throwing water at each other. Buck threw a loaded carbine to him, and he accidentally discharged it into Buck's mouth and killed him. Buck and he had been best friends for a long time and had worked together as a solitary pair for several weeks. He had a clinging attachment to Buck, who was a very self-sufficient and adequate person. He subsequently stated, "Buck was the only person who ever understood or loved me."

Because of the negligence involved in the careless handling of a loaded gun, the patient had a general court martial 3 months later and was sentenced to confinement at hard labor for 3 years. At the time of the court martial he seemed to be struggling to contain his guilt feeling and had only a vague recollection of the details of the accident. However, he was able to maintain good contact with reality until nine months later. At that time he began to ruminate constantly about his offense. Within a few days, he experienced an acute psychotic break. He was transferred to Valley Forge Army Hospital in a very disturbed state. He was crying violently, attempted to strangle himself with his pajamas and then to slash his wrist on the window screen, and was extremely combative. He had visual hallucinations of Buck and carried on long conversations with him. He revealed that at times Buck told him "bad things" and at other times "good things." The "bad things" were that he should kill himself and the "good things" were that he should keep on living. He was given a series of 20 electroconvulsive treatments and experienced a complete remission of his psychosis.

Case 2

While examining a revolver behind the line in Korea, a 20-year-old soldier accidentally discharged the gun, shooting another soldier through the chest and

---

* From Beck and Valin (1953).

killing him. He was sentenced to two years of hard labor for "culpable negligence." Eight months after the accident, while serving his term, he became increasingly upset and had to be hospitalized. He began to engage in obsessive rumination about the accident and in fantasies that would magically undo the deed. Within a few weeks, he became openly psychotic, suicidal, and violent. He had visual and auditory hallucinations involving the dead soldier. He saw the latter coming to him sitting on a cloud and holding a revolver in his left hand. The soldier would upbraid him for what he had done and would then "take off" in reverse. In the course of 20 electroconvulsive treatments, there was complete remission of symptoms.

Case 3

A 22-year-old rifleman accidentally shot his platoon sergeant while on patrol in Korea. He tried to conceal his emotional reaction to the event but a month later he began to hear voices saying, "This is it . . . take a rifle and put a clip in and kill yourself." Another voice then said, "Don't do it, it won't do any good. Then there will be two of you [dead]." At the time of his transfer to Valley Forge Army Hospital he showed moderate agitation, depression, and tremendous anxiety. He frequently expressed the fear of losing his genitalia. In the course of psychotherapy, his symptoms largely abated.

DIFFERENTIAL DIAGNOSIS

In trying to make a distinction between neurotic and psychotic depression, the best guide is to designate as psychotic depressive all cases that show definite signs of psychosis, such as loss of reality, delusions and hallucinations.

Foulds (1960) conducted a systematic study to determine what symptoms differentiated neurotic and psychotic depressives. He administered an inventory of 86 items to 20 neurotic depressives and 20 psychotic depressives, all under 60 years of age. He found that 14 items occurred at least 25 per cent more frequently among the psychotic than among the neurotic group. Using those 14 items as a scale, he was able to sort out correctly 90 per cent of the patients diagnosed clinically as psychotic depressives and 80 per cent of the neurotic depressives. In the list below, the frequency among the psychotics is stated first in the parentheses after each item and that among neurotics is second.

1. He is an unworthy person in his own eyes (12–3).
2. He is a condemned person because of his sins. (12–3).
3. People are talking about him and criticizing him because of things he has done wrong (10–1).
4. He is afraid to go out alone (13–4).
5. He has said things that have injured others (9–2).
6. He is so "worked-up" that he paces about wringing his hands (11–4).

7. He cannot communicate with others because he doesn't seem to be on the same "wave-length" (10–3).
8. There is something unusual about his body, with one side being different from the other, or meaning something different (6–0).
9. The future is pointless (12–7).
10. He might do away with himself because he is no longer able to cope with his difficulties (8–3).
11. Other people regard him as very odd (8–3).
12. He is often bothered with pains over his heart, in his chest, or in his back (8–3).
13. He is so low in spirits that he just sits for hours on end (12–7).
14. When he goes to bed, he wouldn't care if he "never woke up again" (10–5).

Ideas or delusions relevant to being unworthy, condemned, and criticized, and the delusion of being physically altered, are the best differentiators between the two groups.

Aside from delusions, the typical signs and symptoms of depression are found in a large proportion of both neurotic and psychotic depressives. As shown in Table 5–1, the features appear with relatively high frequency in both conditions. This frequency distribution was obtained by abstracting the ratings and diagnoses made by our psychiatrists on a random sample of psychiatric inpatients and outpatients. Each clinical feature was rated according to its severity as absent, mild, moderate, or severe. The records of 50 patients diagnosed as psychotic-depressive reaction and of 50 diagnosed as neurotic-depressive reaction were used in this analysis.

It is apparent that in almost all instances the signs and symptoms of depression were observed in the majority of both neurotic and psychotic depressives. Diurnal variation of mood occurred substantially more frequently among the psychotic depressives, but it was present in only a minority of these cases. Constipation occurred twice as frequently in the psychotic-depressive group as might be expected because the patients in this group were generally in the older age category. Although almost all the clinical features were observed more frequently in the psychotic-depressive group, the disparity in their relative frequency was not marked (with the exception of the two just mentioned).

Since each clinical feature was evaluated not only in terms of presence and absence but also in terms of severity, it was possible to ascertain the relative severity of the specific signs and symptoms in the two groups. It was found that the psychotic depressives tended to show a greater degree of intensity or severity on each of these signs and symptoms. This was expected, since the gobal rating of depth of depression was substantially higher in the psychotic-depressive group. The frequency of *severe* ratings in the two groups is shown in Table 5–1. In every instance, the psychotic-depressive group received substantially more severe ratings than the neurotic group.

It may be concluded that there are no specific signs or symptoms, aside from delusions, that distinguish psychotic from neurotic depressives; and the more severe the symptoms, the more likely a patient is to be diagnosed as a psychotic depressive. These findings tend to support the thesis that, so far as specific depressive symptoms are concerned, the difference between the neurotic and the psychotic depressive reactions is quantitative rather than qualitative.

Part II.
TREATMENT
OF DEPRESSION

Chapter 6.
Pharmacotherapy

Pharmacotherapy for depression is at least as ancient as Homer, who related in *The Odyssey* that Penelope took a drug to dull her grief for her long-absent husband. The two main classes of drugs in use in the treatment of depression today were originally tested in schizophrenic patients but, as in the case of electroconvulsive therapy, were found to be more effective in treating apathy and depression than other clinical symptoms. Iproniazid, in the first major class, was shown to prevent sedation in mice given reserpine; this drug had also been used in the treatment of tuberculosis in 1955, and it was observed to produce a euphoric effect. Interest in imipramine and certain of its derivatives was stimulated because of their structural resemblance to the phenothiazines which had been used successfully in schizophrenia. Iproniazid seemed to be effective in its first tests as an antidepressant, and imipramine given to a large group of patients seemed, to the surprise of investigators, to work far better with predominantly depressive rather than predominantly schizophrenic patients.*

The two new classes of drugs were simultaneously introduced in 1957, and they have stimulated a considerable amount of research and introduction of new drugs since then. The two major classes are: (a) the tricyclics, imipramine, amitriptyline, and closely related compounds, and (b) the monoamine oxidase inhibitors (MAOI), which include tranylcypromine and phenelzine. Lithium carbonate was reported in 1964 for the treatment of mania, but subsequent articles indicate it is useful in treating certain types of depression. Various authors have reviewed controlled studies of antidepressant drugs, for example, Brady,[1] Cole,[2] Hordern,[3] and most recently Klein and Davis.[4] Since the last review, many additional studies have been completed and new drugs introduced (e.g., doxepin). Table 6–1 presents the names and dosages of drugs currently marketed in the United States for the treatment of depression.

This chapter presents an extensive review of articles published through

---

* In order to facilitate reference to the large number of drug studies, the cited articles are listed together *at the end of this chapter.*

Table 6–1.

DRUGS USED IN TREATMENT OF DEPRESSION

Generic name	Trade name	Strength	Effective dose range
Tricyclic Compounds			
Imipramine	Tofranil, Presamine	10 mg., 25 mg., 50 mg.	75–300 mg.
Desipramine	Norpramin, Pertofrane	25 mg., 50 mg.	75–200 mg.
Amitriptyline	Elavil	10 mg., 25 mg., 50 mg.	75–300 mg.
Nortriptyline	Aventyl	10 mg., 25 mg.	20–100 mg.
Protriptyline	Vivactil	5 mg., 10 mg.	15–60 mg.
Doxepin	Sinequan	10 mg., 25 mg., 50 mg.	50–300 mg.
Monoamine Oxidase Inhibitors (MAOI)			
Phenelzine	Nardil	15 mg.	45–75 mg.
Tranylcypromine	Parnate	10 mg.	20–60 mg.
Other			
Methylphenidate	Ritalin	5 mg., 10 mg., 20 mg.	20–60 mg.

October 1972 on the antidepressant drugs. The review includes six tri-cyclic antidepressants; five MAOI drugs; lithium; and methylphenidate (Ritalin).

The search for relevant articles used the following sources: *Index Medicus,* abstracts from the National Clearinghouse for Mental Health, *Excerpta Medica, Psychological Abstracts, Psychopharmacology Abstracts,* and journals known to publish articles on psychopharmacology.

The basic criteria for incuding a study in our analyses were that the study has been controlled—i.e., a comparison of a drug group(s) with a control group(s), either a placebo or another drug—and that patients had been randomly assigned to either group. All studies cited in our tabulations used patients over 18 years of age who manifested depression. Several studies that did not specify characteristics of the patient sample were included because they met the minimal criteria. Studies that included more than one drug trial are tabulated more than once.

Differences in method and patient population may also result in different outcomes with different meanings for each study. The phenomenon of spontaneous improvement should be taken into consideration in evaluating drug results. It has been noted that in the absence of any treatment some patients show marked recovery. This may be related to the type of depression. In studies cited by Klerman and Cole[5] 46 per cent of inpatients with acute disorders showed a positive placebo response as compared with 16 per cent of *chronic* inpatients. When the controls show a high placebo response rate, a drug must be especially potent to register a statistically significant effect. In some cited studies, drug improvement (60-70 per cent) was greater than but not statistically superior to placebo (20-46 per cent) improvement.[4]

Other variables to be considered in analyses of drug vs. placebo, or any other drug study, are: the utilization of a predrug washout period[7] (avoiding contamination or effects of previous medication[34]); the effect of an atropine placebo having possible antidepressant activity: the effect of "cross-over" design; and psychological changes, other than in the level of depression, induced by the drug.[13]

TRICYCLICS

TRICYCLICS VS. PLACEBO

A summary of controlled trials of currently used tricyclics compared with placebo is presented in Table 6–2. The conventional 5 per cent level was used as the criterion of statistical significance. It is apparent from the table that drug treatment in general was superior to placebo.

Table 6–2.
CONTROLLED STUDIES COMPARING TRICYCLICS WITH PLACEBO

Drug studied	INPATIENTS		OUTPATIENTS		MIXED GROUP		TOTAL ALL GROUPS	
	Superior to placebo	Not superior	Superior to placebo	Not superior	Superior to placebo	Not superior	Superior to placebo	Not superior
Imipramine	26	16	6	4	1	3	33	23
Desipramine	3	2	1	0	0	0	4	2
Amitriptyline	7	4	7	2	0	0	14	6
Nortriptyline	4	3	1	0	0	0	5	3
Protriptyline	1	0	2	0	0	0	3	0
Doxepin	1	0	1	0	0	0	2	0
TOTALS	42	25	18	6	1	3	61	34

Out of 67 inpatient trials (61 articles),[19-62, 76-86, 88-92, 94] 42 (63 per cent) showed statistically significant improvement.[19-46, 76-83, 88-89, 94] In 24 trials (20 articles) involving exclusively outpatients[6-15, 67-75, 93] 18 (75 per cent) showed improvement that was statistically significant.[6-11, 63, 67-74, 87, 93] In one out of four trials of mixed inpatients and outpatients, the psychoactive drug was superior to placebo.[16-18, 53]

Differences may be observed in the responses to the individual drugs.* Imipramine[6-62] was significantly superior to placebo in 33 (59 per cent) of the 56 trials,[6-11, 19-46] while amitriptyline[67-86] was reported statistically significant in 14 (70 per cent) of the 20 comparisons.[67-73, 76-83] When their respective derivatives are included in the calculations, this relationship remains about the same: imipramine and its derivative desipramine[23, 36, 63-66] were significantly effective in 60 per cent of the trials; amitriptyline and its derivatives, nortriptyline,[72, 83, 87-92] protriptyline,[87,74] and doxepin[93-94] were significantly effective in 73 per cent of the trials. The derivatives themselves were significantly superior to placebo in 14 out of 19 studies,[63-66, 74, 83, 87-89, 93-94] but the number of studies is too small for any valid comparisons among the specific agents.

IMIPRAMINE VS. AMITRIPTYLINE

Table 6–3 presents a tabulation of controlled studies of imipramine vs. amitriptyline, as well as other drugs. The direct comparison of randomly assigned patient groups treated with different drugs provides reliable information for analysis.

Of the 16 studies comparing imipramine and amitriptyline,[62, 95-109] 38 per cent reported amitriptyline as significantly superior to imipramine,[104-109] while imipramine was superior in 13 per cent of the studies.[95-96] It is possible that differences in the efficacy of these two drugs may be related to the characteristics of the samples. Hordern and his coworkers,[105-107] for instance, found that severely depressed aged females responded significantly better with amitriptyline than with imipramine, especially with respect to depression, associated agitation, and associated insomnia.

Four of the comparative studies used outpatients exclusively: three of these showed no significant difference between the two drugs[97, 102-103] and one reported amitriptyline as significantly superior,[107] but the statistics were insufficient for inpatient-outpatient comparisons.

Although the pooling of heterogeneous data from diverse studies has many inherent flaws, it is sometimes useful to compare the mean scores derived from large numbers of studies in order to highlight gross differences.

---

* The data on imipramine are presented first because this drug was studied the most extensively. Amitriptyline ranked second in the literature in the number of controlled studies.

Based on all studies cited, the mean percentage of patient improvement was approximately 66 per cent with amitriptyline, 61 per cent with imipramine, and 31 per cent with placebo. These figures suggest a substantial superiority of drugs over placebo; they also indicate that at least one out of three patients did not improve on these tricyclics during the period of the drug treatment.

IMIPRAMINE VS. OTHER TRICYCLICS

A summary of controlled studies of imipramine vs. other tricyclics is also contained in Table 6–3. Most of the research, besides comparison of imipramine with amitriptyline, has been concentrated on imipramine's dimethyl derivative, desipramine (Norpramin). Initial interest in desipramine was generated by its rapid effect in many animals, and early investigators also speculated that desipramine was the "active ingredient" in imipramine.[5] Of 12 controlled studies reported,[23, 110-120] two showed imipramine as significantly superior,[23, 110] and 10 found no significant difference in antidepressant activity.[111-120] Five studies reported desipramine as effecting a more rapid onset of improvement, [110-114] but this difference usually disappeared later on. Contrariwise, Waldron and Bates[115] reported desipramine as producing no quicker onset of improvement than an inert placebo; and Heller, Zahourek, and Whittington[23] reported imipramine as significantly faster than desipramine. Thus there may be some differences in the speed of effectiveness.

Comparative studies of imipramine with other tricyclics showed no significant difference vs. nortriptyline,[98, 101, 123] protriptyline,[60, 124] or doxepin.[125-127] Imipramine in comparison with the second class of major antidepressant drugs, the MAOIs, has also received much attention in research. This is discussed in a later section.

AMITRIPTYLINE VS. OTHER TRICYCLICS

A survey of controlled studies comparing amitriptyline with tricyclics other than imipramine is listed in Table 6–4.

Eight studies comparing nortriptyline (Aventyl), a derivative of amitriptyline, have been published. None showed a significant difference in effectiveness between the two drugs.[83, 98, 101, 128-132] Another derivative of amitriptyline, protriptyline (Vivactil) has been compared with its parent drug. In six controlled studies, amitriptyline was statistically superior in two,[133-134] and there was no difference in four. [74, 97, 135-136]

Doxepin (Sinequan), closely resembling amitriptyline in structure, has come on the market more recently. Of the nine reported studies, there was no significant difference between doxepin and amitriptyline in five.[138-142] Doxepin was significantly superior to amitriptyline in three,[143-145] and ami-

Table 6-3.

STUDIES SHOWING IMIPRAMINE SUPERIOR TO, INFERIOR TO, OR EQUIVALENT TO OTHER TRICYCLICS

Comparison Drug	INPATIENTS Imipramine			OUTPATIENTS Imipramine			MIXED Imipramine			TOTAL Imipramine		
	Super.	No Diff.	Infer.	Super.	No Diff.	Infer.	Super.	No Diff.	Infer.	Super.	No Diff.	Infer.
Amitriptyline	1	4	5	0	3	1	1	1	0	2	8	6
Desipramine	2	9	0	0	1	0	0	0	0	2	10	0
Nortriptyline	0	2	0	0	1	0	0	0	0	0	3	0
Protriptyline	0	0	0	0	2	0	0	0	0	0	2	0
Doxepin	0	3	0	0	0	0	0	0	0	0	3	0
TOTALS	3	18	5	0	7	1	1	1	0	4	26	6

Table 6-4.

SURVEY OF STUDIES COMPARING AMITRIPTYLINE WITH OTHER TRICYCLICS

Comparison Drug	INPATIENTS Amitriptyline			OUTPATIENTS Amitriptyline			MIXED Amitriptyline			TOTALS Amitriptyline		
	Super.	No Diff.	Infer.	Super.	No Diff.	Infer.	Super.	No Diff.	Infer.	Super.	No Diff.	Infer.
Imipramine	5	4	1	1	3	0	0	0	1	6	7	2
Desipramine	0	0	0	0	0	0	0	1	0	0	1	0
Nortriptyline	0	5	0	0	0	0	0	3	0	2	8	0
Protriptyline	0	2	0	2	2	0	0	0	0	0	4	0
Doxepin	1	2	1	0	2	2	0	1	0	1	5	3
TOTALS	6	13	2	3	7	2	0	5	1	9	25	5

triptyline was significantly superior in one.[137] Three studies[138-139, 144] reported an antianxiety effect of doxepin, as well as antidepressant activity.

Finally, one study in which amitriptyline and desipramine were compared reported no difference between the two.[96]

OTHER TRICYCLICS AND RELATED ANTIDEPRESSANTS

Very few studies have compared the derivatives of imipramine or amitriptyline with one another. Those reported were nortriptyline vs. desipramine[146-147] and protriptyline vs. desipramine.[148] None of the studies showed significant differences between the two drugs compared.

Other tricyclic-type drugs in various stages of investigation are not available on the U.S. market at the present time. These include opipramol (Insidon), trimipramine (Surmontil), and iprindole.

Seven controlled studies have been reported on opipramol.[22, 116, 149-153] Of these, six compared the drug with placebo. Opipramol was significantly superior in three,[149-151] and there was no difference in three.[22, 116, 152] Two reported no difference when opipramol was compared with imipramine,[22, 116] and one study reported amitriptyline to be significantly superior to opipramol.[153]

Trimipramine was also found to have measurable antidepressant effects. Two studies reported trimipramine superior to placebo,[73, 154] four showed no measurable difference between trimipramine and amitriptyline,[73, 155-157] and two reported trimipramine significantly superior to imipramine.[121-122] In the studies comparing trimipramine and amitriptyline, more cross-validation and comparable dosage experiments are needed before any definitive conclusions can be made as to their differences in sedation and rapidity of action.[4]

Finally, iprindole, a drug closely related to doxepin, was found superior to placebo in three studies.[158-160]

MONOAMINE OXIDASE INHIBITORS

Monoamine oxidase inhibitors (MAOIs) constitute the second major group of antidepressant drugs. Within the MAOI category a further division is commonly made, according to structure. These subgroups are the hydrazines (isocarboxazid, nialamide, and phenelzine [Nardil]) and the nonhydrazines (tranylcypromine [Parnate] and pargyline). As of January 31, 1973, only phenelzine and tranylcypromine are approved for use in the United States as antidepressants.

MAOIs vs. PLACEBO

Isocarboxazid[15, 21, 24, 59-60, 91, 161-164] was superior to placebo in two out of 11 controlled studies reported.[24, 161] In six controlled studies, nialamide was not statistically superior to placebo.[15, 165-169] Phenelzine[18-19, 21, 61, 164, 172, 176-179] was reported as more effective than placebo in six out of 10 studies.[19, 172, 176-179] Pargyline (two out of two studies),[170-171] and tranylcypromine (three out of four studies)[172-175] seem to be effective antidepressants, although the number of studies is small.

MAOIs vs. Tricyclics

The tricyclic most extensively compared with MAOIs is imipramine. No study has shown an MAOI drug to be significantly superior to imipramine. In 17 studies (25 trials) there was no significant difference between the MAOI drug and imipramine.[15, 19, 59-61, 102, 180, 182, 184-192] In nine studies (11 trials) imipramine was superior.[18, 20-21, 95-96, 180-183] Tranylcypromine was the only MAOI that was not inferior to imipramine in at least one study.[102, 180, 192]

Hays[91] found no significant difference between isocarboxazid and nortriptyline in depressed patients. Two studies compared amitriptyline with isocarboxazid, but other drugs were also involved.[96, 102] Both studies reported no significant difference in the rate of remission.

COMPARISON OF DRUG AND ELECTROCONVULSIVE THERAPIES

Electroconvulsive therapy (ECT), in use almost three times longer than modern antidepressant drug treatment, remains a vital tool in the treatment of hospitalized severe depressives. Seven controlled studies comparing imipramine with ECT have been reported. Of these, three studies showed ECT to be significantly superior to imipramine,[33, 193-194] and four reported nonsignificant trends between the two.[18, 28, 51, 195] The other drug to which ECT has been compared was phenelzine. In all three studies ECT was significantly superior to phenelzine.[194, 196-197]

Although the speed of action was significantly faster for ECT in all studies, relapse rates were reported as higher with ECT as opposed to imipramine, phenelzine, and other tricyclics. One way to prevent this is drug maintenance therapy after discontinuation of ECT treatments.[28] A 6-month follow-up study by Imlah, Ryan, and Harrington[19] found that only 15 per cent of the patients on drug maintenance with imipramine or phenelzine had relapsed; whereas 51 per cent with no drug maintenance had relapsed.

LITHIUM

Lithium is the lightest alkali metal in the periodic table and is used mainly in the management of mania and manic-depressive psychosis. Its form in treatment is a lithium salt or lithium ion, and its therapeutic action is found to be twofold: prophylactic and curative. The efficacy of lithium in the treatment and management of mania appears to be in the range of 44–100 per cent effective within 5–10 days from onset of treatment.[4] Recently researchers have been investigating lithium's use and effectiveness with primary depressive illness.

TREATMENT OF DEPRESSION WITH LITHIUM

Five controlled studies dealing with lithium's efficacy in the treatment of depression have been published.[52, 198-202] In an early study[198] with a small sample of 12 patients with acute depression, no significant difference between lithium and placebo was found. Goodwin, Murphy, and Bunney[199] compared lithium and a placebo in 30 hospitalized depressives, in a unique longitudinal design which switched patients between lithium and placebo. Although the drug was more effective in mania, depressed patients with a cyclic history responded more favorably than nonpolar patients. The latter trend was not significant.

Fieve, Platman, and Plutchik[52] conducted a study comparing lithium with imipramine in 29 acutely depressed patients diagnosed as manic-depressives. Although the measured changes were significantly greater in the imipramine group, both groups showed improvement. It was concluded that lithium, though weak, possessed some antidepressant quality. Platman[200] compared lithium with imipramine in 70 manic-depressives. Imipramine was significantly superior to lithium treatment in depression, while the reverse was true in mania. Finally, in a double-blind study by Mendels, Secunda, and Dyson,[201] lithium was compared to desipramine in 24 acutely depressed patients. They found that both agents exhibited antidepressant activities, but no significant difference was found between the two. These studies also allude to the possible connection or similarity of mania and depression.

PROPHYLAXIS OF DEPRESSION

Because of the "dual action" of lithium, the majority of research has centered on lithium as a preventative agent in mania and depression. Coppen *et al.*[202] compared prophylactic administration of lithium with a placebo in a group of 65 patients with recurrent affective disorders. It was found that patients (globally rated) on maintenance lithium were significantly better than placebo patients (86 per cent vs. 8 per cent). Also, contrary to Goodwin *et al.,*[199] the nature of the disorder (unipolar vs. bipolar) had no relation to lithium's effectiveness. Schou[203] studied 34 patients randomly assigned to lithium or placebo. More than half of the placebo group relapsed, as compared to none in the lithium group. Angst *et al.*[204] compared lithium and nonlithium treatment periods in a staistical analysis of 244 patients as their own controls. The results showed a significant reduction in frequency of hospital readmission.

Polackova, Billy, and Hanus[205] did a comparative study of lithium vs. placebo, each group containing 15 patients. In this longitudinal design, they found no statistically significant decrease with respect to the number of depressive phases recurring in the lithium group as compared with placebo. In another controlled study, Melia[206] compared lithium and placebo in 18 patients. The difference in the number of patients who relapsed was not significant ($p < .10$), but the average length of remission was 433 days for lithium patients, 244 for the placebo group, a significant difference. Finally, Fieve, Platman, and Plutchik[207] found no significant difference in the frequency of recurrence of depressive episodes between patients on extended lithium treatments vs. those on lithium for a shorter time (4 months) who were switched to imipramine or placebo (36 on lithium, 10 on imipramine, 6 on placebo).

Thus, in six controlled studies, lithium was significantly superior to placebo in three[202-205] and not significantly superior in three.[205-207] Clearly, the specific application of lithium to the treatment of depression is an open question which requires further research.

CONTRAINDICATIONS, WARNINGS, PRECAUTIONS, ADVERSE EFFECTS

The following section presents an overview of the contraindications, warnings, precautions, and adverse effects of tricyclic and MAOI drugs and lithium. The physician should consult the FDA approved informational circulars distributed by drug companies before prescribing a specific drug. Since these circulars are modified periodically, it is necessary to refer to the most recent version in order to obtain up-to-date information. In addition, the *FDA Drug Bulletin* should be consulted for important prescribing information. This section is intended to acquaint the physician with possible drug hazards but not to act as a substitute for the detailed information provided by the drug companies and the FDA.

TRICYCLICS

Contraindications

All tricyclics are contraindicated when an MAOI is being given or when MAOI therapy has been discontinued less than 2 weeks prior. A tricyclic should not be given during the acute recovery period after myocardial infarction. It is also contraindicated with patients who exhibited previous hypersensitivity to it.

Warnings

Tricyclic antidepressants have been reported to produce sinus tachycardia, arrhythmias, and prolonged conduction time; consequently, if tricyclics are administered to patients with cardiovascular disorders or a history of seizures, they should be watched carefully. The antihypertensive action of guanethidine may be blocked by tricyclics. Also, because of the anticholinergic activity of the tricyclics, caution should be used in patients subject to glaucoma or a history of urinary retention.

The ability to perform hazardous tasks (e.g., operation of motor vehicle) may be impaired because of decreased mental and/or physical functioning.

The safe use of antidepressants by patients during pregnancy or lactation or by children under the age of 12 has not yet been established.

Precautions

Possible suicide in depressed patients who have not yet remitted remains a danger, and this type of patient should not be allowed to possess large quantities of the drugs. Manic-depressive patients may shift to the manic phase, and schizophrenics may experience an exaggeration of their symptoms following the use of tricyclics.

The hazards of therapy may be increased when tricyclics are used concomitantly with ECT. Alcohol and barbiturate responses may be enhanced by tricyclics.

Adverse Effects

Several methodological problems exist when one evaluates drug side effects. Busfield, Schneller, and Capra[208] compared the incidence of complaints recorded prior to treatment with treatment "side effects" in isocarboxazid, phenelzine, and imipramine. They found that 87 per cent of the "apparent" drug-related side effects had been recorded prior to treatment. Rickels, Ward, and Schut[11] found differential tolerance of side effects dependent upon the patient's socioeconomic status and type of treatment center. Thus, reported side effects may be variable for reasons other than type of drug and dosage level. Common side effects (5–30 per cent of patients treated) reported with imipramine, amitriptyline, and the other tricyclics were dry mouth, sweating, mild tremor of the upper extremities, nausea, vomiting, constipation, drowsiness, visual distortions, and rashes.[49, 106-107, 109, 194] These were usually less with the derivative tricyclics than with their parent compounds.

A few cases using imipramine reported a small incidence of jaundice (0.5–1 per cent), leukopenia, leukocytosis, agranulocytosis, and occasional eosinophilia.[4, 5, 209, 214] Agitation and insomnia have also been reported with initial use of imipramine and protriptyline, but amitriptyline appeared to be more sedating in that respect.[4, 5] The specific cardiovascular problems with imipramine and amitriptyline, more so with the former, were hypotension and tachycardia (5 per cent).[215-216] Rare but more serious effects reported with imipramine were pulmonary emboli,[217-219] myocardial infarctions,[219-221] and congestive heart failure.[218-219, 222] It is undetermined whether these effects are due to the drug itself or the patient's past history and predisposition.

Withdrawal side effects were reported with abrupt cessation of imipramine treatment.[223]

The skin, cardiovascular, and central nervous system side effects might be due to the anticholinergic properties of the tricyclics. Decreasing the dosage usually diminished the side effects.[224]

MAOI DRUGS

Since only phenelzine (Nardil) and tranylcypromine (Parnate) are available as MAOI antidepressants in the United States, the following section is restricted to only those drugs.

Contraindications

Tranylcypromine and phenelzine are contraindicated in patients with cardiovascular disorders, cerebrovascular defects, or pheochromocytoma. These drugs should not be administered in conjunction with or following other MAOI inhibitors, with tricyclics, or with sympathomimetic drugs. Patients should be instructed as to certain foods that should be avoided, such as cheese, beer, wines, pickled herring, and other foods with a high tyramine content. The MAOIs should not be used with CNS depressants, such as alcohol, narcotics, or hypotensive agents.

Warnings

The safe use of MAOIs during pregnancy and lactation and by young children has not yet been established. Patients should also be warned about taking nonprescription drugs when on MAOI therapy. Hypertensive crises may result if diet is not properly maintained. MAOIs may suppress anginal pain warning of myocardial ischemia.

Precautions

Tranylcypromine and phenelzine should not be used with ECT. Moreover, suicidal risk should be considered and adequate precautions taken whenever dealing with depressed patients. Hypotension has been reported; and if it occurs, dosages should be adjusted. Pre-existing symptoms such as anxiety and agitation may be aggravated by MAOI drugs. Precautions should be taken with epileptic patients because of the MAOI drugs' influence on convulsive thresholds in animal experiments. Also, MAOI therapy should be discontinued 7 days before elective surgery.

Adverse Reactions

Similar skin and CNS side effects have been reported with the MAOIs as well as the tricyclics, but they were generally more numerous and more severe with the MAOIs. These included dizziness, dry mouth, constipation, impotence, orthostatic hypotension, and paroxysmal hypertension.

Two more serious syndromes produced by MAOIs were headaches and hypertension ("cheese reaction"), which were later found to be related to the patient's diet. This reaction, too, varied with the individual being treated.[225]

LITHIUM

Lithium carbonate can produce a wide range of effects from very mild to very severe. It is a relatively safe drug when properly prescribed and lithium blood serum levels are monitored (<1.5 mEq/Liter).[4]

Contraindications of lithium carbonate include its use in patients with evidence of brain damage, or notable renal or cardiovascular disease. Lithium use during pregnancy is contraindicated.

Lithium therapy must be discontinued if signs of lithium toxicity are present. These include nausea, vomiting, drowsiness, muscle weakness, or lack of coordination. Information as to the safety of lithium's use in young children has not yet been established.

Patients must maintain a normal diet with adequate fluid (2500–3000 ml.) and salt intake. Higher susceptibility to lithium toxicity is noted with increased sweating or diarrhea, and the diet should be adjusted.

Toxic reaction and side effects are related to the patient's blood serum level of lithium. Side effects include nausea, ataxia, anorexia, vomiting, hypertonic muscles, confusion, seizures, somnolence, and stupor.

METHYLPHENIDATE

Common adverse reactions are insomnia and nervousness. These can usually be controlled by removing evening or afternoon administration and also reducing the dosage. Other side effects include hypersensitivity, skin rash, nausea, dizziness, anorexia, palpitations, headache, drowsiness, pressure and pulse changes, cardiac arrhythmia, angina, tachycardia, and abdominal pain. These effects occur more frequently in children after prolonged therapy. Drug dependence and toxic psychosis have been reported in those patients with predisposed personality types.

MANAGEMENT OF SIDE EFFECTS

The management of side effects is based on clinical experience more than on systematic studies.* The most common side effects of the tricyclics are related to the anticholinergic actions of this drug. Most patients complain of dryness of the mouth—although studies have shown that decreased salivation appears in many patients who are not on medication. In any event, even though dryness of the mouth is irritating, the patient should generally be encouraged to ignore it or accept it as a minor effect of a powerful drug.

Constipation is another frequent effect of antidepressant medication. This particular symptom may be treated in the same way that constipation is generally treated. Certain foods or medical preparations that increase bulk may be prescribed. Mineral oil or bowel stimulants such as prune juice may be recommended. For more intractable constipation, one of the saline cathartics such as Milk of Magnesia may be prescribed.

Gastrointestinal disturbances other than constipation may occur but usually disappear within a week. Persistence of nausea, vomiting, abdominal pain, or diarrhea might indicate an idiosyncratic or allergic reaction. In such a case, the physician should consider substitution of an alternate preparation.

Increased perspiration occasionally accompanied by flushing is fairly common with the use of tricyclics and may come on in attacks lasting from 5 to 20 minutes. Since the patient can usually be encouraged to tolerate the symptom, its occurrence is generally not an indication for discontinuation of the drug.

Delayed micturition is apt to be a more serious complication since it can result in urinary retention. Elderly patients with a history of disease of the genital-urinary tract should be carefully watched. The underlying genital-urinary problem should be relieved if possible. If the complication persists, the physician should change from a tricyclic drug to an MAOI since urinary retention is less frequent with the latter group of drugs.

Orthostatic hypotension is not unusual in the first few weeks of treatment with a tricyclic or an MAOI. The drop in systolic and diastolic pressure averages about 10 per cent. Usually this symptom disappears in less than a month and can be controlled by instructing the patient how to adjust to postural changes. The patient with this symptom should be cautioned against rising abruptly or standing in one place for a prolonged period of time. By getting up slowly from the lying or sitting position, and by shifting

* The reader is referred for more detailed information to Kline's monograph.[226]

his weight from one foot to the other while standing, he can help to counteract the effects of drop in blood pressure.

Dizziness, vertigo, and fainting may occur even in the absence of hypotension. When these side effects occur, they tend to appear during the early part of treatment. If the physician considers these side effects detrimental, he should reduce the dosage of the drug. If the symptoms do not disappear within a week after this regimen, then an alternate medication should be substituted.

Fatigue, lethargy, drowsiness, and weakness may occur during the early phase of treatment but usually disappear within 10 days or 2 weeks.

Overstimulation, jitteriness, and agitation may also be side effects of the drug or may be manifestations of the depression. If these symptoms become marked, the utilization of a mild sedative with the concomitant administration of a phenothiazine may be considered. Substitution of an MAOI might be considered since these side effects are less frequent with the MAOI drugs.

Certain neurological effects such as tremors, nystagmus, muscle twitching, paresthesias, tinnitus, and neuritis have been reported. Sedatives, an antihistamine, or a mild phenothiazine may be considered to counteract these symptoms. Other, more severe manifestations of central nervous system toxicity, such as memory impairment, ataxia, confusion, delirium or hallucinations, are indications for discontinuing the medication. Since memory impairment may be one of the characteristics of depression, this particular symptom should be a warning only if it becomes progressively worse.

Headache also occurs frequently in depression and may be incorrectly attributed to the medication. If there is no contraindication to their use, ordinary analgesics may be prescribed.

Optical difficulties, particularly for tasks requiring near vision, sometimes occur because of the accommodation difficulty. It may be necessary to prescribe glasses or change the present prescription in order to compensate for this difficulty. The optical problem clears up when the medication is discontinued.

The tricyclic drugs may reduce the epileptic threshold, and an increase in anticonvulsive medication may be indicated for epileptic patients.

Some patients manifest skin sensitivity beyond simple perspiration and flushing. An idiosyncratic rash that appears to be on an allergic basis can frequently be handled with an antihistamine. If evidence of a serious systemic allergic reaction becomes apparent, then it may be necessary to switch to an alternate preparation. Among the sexual disturbances, which compound the loss of libido generally associated with depression, are impotence and delayed ejaculation. These symptoms generally clear up after several weeks, but if they are particularly troublesome to the patient, it may be necessary to substitute a different medication.

The handicaps produced by the side effects must be weighed against the positive effects of the drugs. As with the other side effects, the persistence, disability, or distress may be sufficient to warrant a change to another drug.

The MAOI drugs may produce practically all the same side effects just noted as characteristic of the tricyclics. In addition, the MAOI drugs may produce severe hypertension. This occurs when the patient is taking foods containing amines that elevate the blood pressure, such as tyramine. Such an effect indicates that this patient is one of those susceptible to "cheese reactions," and it is necessary to discontinue the MAOI and switch to an alternate form of treatment.

Evidence of liver damage is an indication for stopping the medication until the etiology of the disorder has been ascertained.

DOSAGE AND ADMINISTRATION OF ANTIDEPRESSANT DRUGS

Tricyclics

In general, the initial dosage of the tricyclics should be at a low level and then increased to the point of maximal effectiveness if no clinical response is evident and the patient can tolerate the side effects. For tricyclics (except nortriptyline and protriptyline, which have lower dosages), the initial dosage for adult outpatients is 25 mg. three times a day and can be increased to a total of 150 mg. a day. Larger total dosages up to 300 mg. a day may be administered to severely ill, hospitalized patients. Because of the sedative effects, the increases are preferably made in the late afternoon or evening.

Maintenance dosages vary from a total of 40 mg. to 100 mg. a day. When the patient has maintained satisfactory improvement for several weeks, the dosage may be reduced to a level that will maintain relief of symptoms. In order to minimize the probability of a relapse, maintenance therapy should be continued for 3 to 6 months. Treatment should not be terminated abruptly, but the dosage should be gradually tapered off.

Lower dosages are generally indicated for adolescent and elderly patients. Dosages should be initiated at a low level for these patients (e.g., 10 mg. twice a day) and gradually increased until a therapeutic response is noted. In general, total dosage should not exceed 50–75 mg. a day.

MAOI Drugs

Tranylcypromine has a starting dosage of 20 mg. per day, which may be continued for 2 weeks. If there are no signs of a positive response, dosage may be increased to 30 mg. a day. If no clinical response occurs after another week, beneficial action is unlikely. Higher dosages may be more effective, but they increase the likelihood of adverse effects. Maintenance dosage is 10–20 mg. a day.

The initial dosage of phenelzine is 45 mg. a day. This may be gradually increased to 75 mg. a day if necessary to achieve maximal effect. Maintenance dosage is 15 mg. a day.

The same principles regarding maintenance dosage and tapering off apply to the MAOI drugs as to the tricyclics.

LITHIUM CARBONATE

The initial dosage is 300 mg. three times a day for the first day. The total dosage is then increased by 300 mg. daily until noticeable improvement occurs or the serum lithium level reaches 1.5 mEq/Liter.

The administration of lithium carbonate should be conducted under the supervision of a physician experienced in its application and knowledgeable about its side effects. Furthermore, careful laboratory and clinical control is necessary. Prior to treatment, a complete physical examination accompanied by certain electrolyte studies, urinalysis, electrocardiogram, and other blood studies including blood urea nitrogen should be performed. Facilities for prompt and accurate serum lithium determinations must be readily available. Problems regarding optimum dose, maintenance dose, and prophylactic dose should be resolved by specialists in lithium administration. Because of the side effects and toxicity, the necessity for close supervision and clinical control must be continually stressed.

METHYLPHENIDATE

Initial dose is 5 mg. two or three times a day. The last dose should be taken before 2 P.M. The dosage may be increased up to 40 mg. If the patient shows signs of overstimulation, the dosage should be reduced.

CLINICAL APPLICATIONS

When we consider the practical application of the systematic studies of the antidepressant drugs to clinical practice, we find that there are few hard and fast rules. The controlled studies have been designed primarily to determine the efficacy of the drugs in heterogeneous groups of depressed patients and have provided only minimal reliable data to aid in deciding the treatment of choice for a particular individual. Moreover, various studies have sometimes been contradictory in answer to questions such as the preferred drug for endogenous vs. reactive depression and psychotic vs. neurotic depression.

In extracting the relevant information from the reviewed studies, certain generalizations can be made. These have to be adapted and modified in making the final clinical decision for a particular case. In making an initial judgment as to whether a major antidepressant drug (tricyclic, MAOI, lithium) should be prescribed, there is a general clinical consensus that such treatment is specifically indicated in clear-cut moderate or severe depressions of at least several days' duration. Conditions that do not warrant the prescription of an antidepressant include the normal grief reaction following a bereavement or sadness following a disappointment. The major antidepressant drugs are indicated only if these reactions are prolonged and develop into a typical depression. Sadness or low mood, in itself, is not sufficient to warrant administration of these drugs. The patient should manifest pathology in several components of the depressive constellation to justify the drugs: these areas of psychopathology have been outlined in Chapter 2, Symptomatology of Depression. Briefly, they include change in mood (sadness, apathy, crying spells, loss of mirth response), motivational changes (suicidal wishes, wishes to avoid routine activities), cognitive changes (unwarranted pessimism, unrealistically low self-esteem), vegetative changes (disturbance in sleep and loss of appetite), and behavioral changes (retardation or agitation). Questionnaires such as the Depression Inventory[227] or the Self-Rating Depression Scale[228] can be used as a guide in determining the presence and severity of depression.

Ordinarily, mild depressions do not require the use of the major antidepressant drugs. These are often of short duration and apparently respond well to psychological interventions such as empathy, reassurance, and ventilation of feeling by the patient. In 1930, before the advent of specific antidepressants or specialized psychotherapy, Paskind[229] noted that the median duration of depressions seen in psychiatric office practice was 3 months. More recently, Porter[14] reported in a placebo-controlled drug study of general practice patients that, in almost all cases, the depression had remitted within 3 weeks of the first visit. These contrasting findings suggest that depressions referred to psychiatrists tend to be more pronounced than those seen by general practitioners. It is also significant that Porter found imipramine to be no more effective than placebo in his G. P. cases. Similarly, Downing and Rickels[67] found that drug-placebo differences were greater in more severely than in less severely ill depressed outpatients. It might be expected that a larger proportion of depressed patients seen in psychiatric practice is likely to be candidates for vigorous antidepressant treatment than in general practice.

It should be borne in mind that untreated depressions generally start as mild and become progressively worse until they "bottom out" and begin to improve. Consequently, active intervention is indicated if an initially mild depression continues on a downhill course. Similarly, a patient with recurrent severe depressions may be started on an antidepressant medica-

tion earlier than a patient in the initial phase of his first depression. Brief psychotherapy, possibly in conjunction with a "minor" antidepressant such as methylphenidate, seems to be helpful in mild depressions.

Having established that a depression is of sufficient severity or duration to warrant the major antidepressant drugs, the clinician has to decide which of the categories of antidepressants to select. The consensus among the authorities is that the tricyclics are preferable to the MAOI drugs. The main reason for this preference is that considerable vigilance regarding diet is necessary to avoid the possibility of the "cheese reaction" to the MAOIs. Also, the range of MAOI incompatibility with ingredients of over-the-counter drugs is so broad as to increase the likelihood of combinations of incompatible drugs. Furthermore, if the MAOI is discontinued because of lack of response or adverse side effects, the patient will have to wait 2 weeks until starting on a tricyclic. There is less likelihood of an adverse reaction in switching from a tricyclic to an MAOI and no waiting period and minimal likelihood of an adverse reaction in changing from one tricyclic to another.

There are no absolute rules as to the drug of choice within the tricyclic group. The available controlled studies appear to favor amitriptyline over imipramine (Tables 6–2 and 6–3), but the differences are not great and further studies are required to determine the drug of choice for a particular group. The other tricyclics on the market are also effective but, again, further comparative studies are required to establish their relative potency and frequency of side effects. Because of their sedative action, amitriptyline, nortriptyline, or doxepin may be chosen in cases in which insomnia is an important component of the depression. On the other hand, the physician may find it preferable to perscribe a drug with less likelihood of producing drowsiness (e.g., imipramine or desipramine) if the patient is involved in activities requiring alertness (for example, driving a car). Protriptyline is said to have activating properties and may be indicated in cases marked by retardation. Doxepin evidently has specific antianxiety effects and may be chosen in cases in which anxiety is a notable concomitant of depression.

A certain amount of trial and error is necessary in selecting the appropriate medication for a given patient. Lack of noticeable improvement at the end of 2 weeks frequently indicates that the patient is unlikely to respond favorably to that drug in the prescribed dosage. The physician can either increase the dosage or switch to another drug if the patient has already been receiving maximal dosage. In any event, 4 weeks seems to be a good cut-off point if the patient is not responding to a particular drug.

As indicated previously, about one-third of the patients started on a specific tricyclic did not respond during 4 weeks of the trials. However, a body of clinical evidence suggests that certain patients show a high degree of response specificity. In recurrent depressions, they are likely to respond better to one drug than to any of the others. This observation is supported by the report that during the period when tranylcypromine was temporarily taken off the market, some patients who had been switched to other drugs did not show a positive response, and in some cases became worse following the change. When tranylcypromine was reintroduced, they again showed a positive response.[4] Hence, if a patient is intolerant of the side effects of a given drug or is refractory to it, he should be given another drug, ECT, or psychotherapy.

DRUG OR ELECTROCONVULSIVE THERAPY?

There is substantial evidence that many depressions that are refractory to a major antidepressant drug respond to ECT. The British cooperative study[18] indicated that about 50 per cent of the patients who had failed to respond to imipramine subsequently showed a favorable response to ECT. Similarly, it has been found that patients not responding to other tricyclic drugs and MAOIs have responded to ECT.

There seems to be an argument in favor of using ECT with patients who are refractory or hypersensitive to antidepressant drugs or who for some reason refuse to take the medication.

When is ECT indicated as the initial treatment of choice? In making such a decision, the physician must weigh a number of factors. ECT, especially when administered with the modern modifications, is a safe procedure (Chapter 7) but probably not as safe as drug therapy. The evidence already cited indicates that ECT is probably superior to the antidepressants in terms of the proportion of patients benefited and the speed of action. It may be possible to define certain subgroups of depressed patients who are dramatically and rapidly helped by ECT, whereas their response to antidepressant drugs may be delayed for several weeks and may not show the same degree of responsiveness. Mendels[230] and others have defined "predictors" of good ECT response. These predictors in general are typical features of endogenous depression (Chapter 4). The disadvantage of ECT is that the relapse rate is greater following ECT than during treatment with maintenance antidepressant drugs. In addition, ECT produces some degree of confusion and recent memory loss. Unilateral ECT diminishes these side effects.

Other factors must be weighed in making the decision to give ECT. The patient often has a great apprehension of ECT and his family may have an aversion to this form of therapy. This factor might favor using an antidepressant drug initially. Under some circumstances, ECT might require hospitalization; whereas it might be possible to use an antidepressant drug for the same patient on an ambulatory basis. Of course, many patients do receive ECT on an ambulatory outpatient basis.

Putting together the various pros and cons, it seems that the major indications for ECT are as follows: first, it is indicated for use as an "emergency measure" in patients who are severely depressed and highly suicidal.

In such cases, ECT may rapidly alleviate the intense suffering and reduce the suicidal risk. This is a humane remedy for severe depressions that may show a notable response after the first few ECT treatments. Another indication for ECT is the group of patients who have been shown to be refractory to antidepressant drugs, hypersensitive to them, or unwilling to take them.

There seem to be strong objections to ECT amony many physicians and patients. These objections have to be taken into account in making a decision that may require coercion and involuntary commitment in order to be implemented. Moreover, the amnesia and confusion following ECT may make this form of treatment less attractive than drugs.

In view of the evidence of a higher relapse rate after ECT than after drug therapy, it is advisable to prescribe maintenance antidepressant drugs for 6 to 12 months after the termination of ECT.

As will be noted in the chapter on ECT, many clinicians prefer to reserve ECT for desperate or intractable cases, whereas others consider it the treatment of choice for all severe depressions. However, it is apparent from the widespread use of antidepressant drugs and the diminishing use of ECT that the physicians generally prefer drugs to ECT for treating depressions.

LITHIUM

Lithium is still in the experimental phases insofar as the clear definition of its application to depression is concerned. In view of the contradictory findings of the controlled studies, it has not found a place among the other antidepressants as a standard treatment for depression. There is some evidence that it may be more potent than the tricyclics in the depressive phase of manic-depressive disorders, and, therefore, it could well be the drug of choice in a patient who has had prior manic episodes—especially if these responded to lithium. However, since the bipolar depressions constitute only a small fraction of the depressions seen in hospitals, the drug would seem to have a limited applicability. However, it might be used in patients refractory to the other drugs.

With lithium considerably more supervision and laboratory tests are required than with the tricyclics. This might be a disadvantage for patients treated on an ambulatory basis—especially if the laboratory facilities are not readily available. It is apparent that more study and experience with this drug are necessary before its status as an antidepressant can be established.

METHYLPHENIDATE

Methylphenidate has not proven itself to be effective in full-blown clinical depressions. However, it may have an application in mild depressions and in reactive depressions following a serious trauma such as a bereavement or a disappointment in interpersonal relations, etc. Such conditions have been labeled "disappointment dysphorias" by Klein and Davis.[4]

A study by Rickels *et al.*[231] indicates that methylphenidate was more effective than placebo in lower class patients attending a clinic in a city hospital. This medication might be specifically effective in the treatment of mild depressions characterized by apathy and a sense of fatigue. It is possible that a good part of the response is a "placebo effect." However, the combination of a kindly attitude by the physician and a drug that has some stimulant properties may be important in alleviating the patient's distress.

Unfortunately, tolerance may develop rapidly, thus requiring an increasing dosage. The possibility of addiction should be kept in mind.[4] Further studies are necessary to pinpoint the specific value of this drug in mild depressions.

Psychotherapy Combined with Drug Therapy

It has not been possible to perform studies of psychotherapy that possess the elegance characteristic of drug studies. Obviously, such features as the homogeneity of the therapeutic agent, double-blind controls, etc., are not possible. Nonetheless, there is some evidence that a combination of psychotherapy and drug therapy is more effective than drug therapy alone.[232]

REFERENCES

(1) Brady, J.P. (1963): Review of controlled studies of imipramine. Unpublished study.

(2) Cole, J.O. (1964): The therapeutic efficacy of antidepressant drugs: a review. *J. Amer. Med. Ass.* 190(5): 448–455.

(3) Hordern, A. (1965): The antidepressant drugs. *New Eng. J. Med.* 272: 1159–1169.

(4) Klein, D.F. and Davis, J.M. (1969): Diagnosis and drug treatment of psychiatric disorders. (*Baltimore*) *Chapter VII:* 187–298.

(5) Klerman, G.L. and Cole, J.O. (1965): Clinical pharmacology of imipramine and related antidepressant compounds. *Pharmacol. Rev.* 17: 101–141.

(6) Abraham, H.C., Kanter, V.B., and Rosen, I. (1963): A controlled clinical trial of imipramine (Tofranil) with outpatients. *Brit. J. Psychiat.* 109: 286–293.

(7) Ainslie, J.D., Jones, M.B., and Stiefel, J.R. (1965): Practical drug evaluation method: imipramine in depressed outpatients. *Arch. Gen. Psychiat.* 12: 368–373.

(8) Jones, M.B. and Ainslie, J.D. (1966): Value of placebo washout. *Dis. Nerv. Syst.* 27(6): 393–396.

(9) Uhlenhuth, E.H. and Park, L.C. (1963): The influence of medication (imipramine) and doctor in relieving depressed psychoneurotic outpatients. *J. Psychiat, Res.* 2(2): 101–102.

(10) Ball, J.R.B. and Kiloh, L.G. (1959): A controlled trial of imipramine in treatment of depressive states. *Brit. Med. J.* 2: 1052–1055.

(11) Rickels, K., Ward, C.H., and Schut, L. (1964): Different populations, different drug responses: a comparative study of two antidepressants, each used in two different patient groups. *Amer. J. Med. Sci.* 247: 328–335.

(12) Bassa, D.M., Vora, H.D., and Dip, D.W. (1965): Evaluation of efficacy of imipramine in depressive disorders: a double-blind study. *Amer. J. Psychiat.* 121: 1116–1177.

(13) DiMascio, A., Meyer, R.E., and Stifler, L. (1968): Effects of imipramine on individuals varying in level of depression. *Amer. J. Psychiat.* 124: 55–58.

(14) Porter, A.M. (1970): Depressive illness in a general practice. A demographic study and a controlled trial of imipramine. *Brit. Med. J.* 1: 773–778.

(15) Schorer, C.E., Lowinger, P., and Dobie, S. (1966): The real effect of imipramine, isocarboxazid and nialamide. *Mich. Med.* 65: 1071–1075.

(16) Azcarate, C.A. (1969): Experimental study with a new antidepressant (Thiazesein QS10496). Controlled study with imipramine and placebo. *Rev. Neuropsiquiat.* 32: 194–211.

(17) Malitz, S., Wilkens, B., and Esecover, H. (1959): Preliminary evaluation of Tofranil in a combined inpatient and outpatient setting. *Canad. Psych. Ass. J.* 4(Suppl): S152–157.

(18) Clinical Psychiatry Committee of the Medical Research Council (1965): Clinical trial of the treatment of depressive illness. *Brit. Med. J.* 5439: 881–886.

(19) Imlah, N.W., Ryan, E., and Harrington, J.A. (1965): The influence of antidepressant drugs on the response to ECT and on subsequent relapse rates. In Bradley, P.B. and Bente, D. (Eds.) *Neuropsychopharm*, 4: 438–442.

(20) Overall, J.E., Hollister, L.E., Pokorny, A.D., Casey, J.F., and Katz, G. (1962): Drug therapy in depressions, controlled evaluation of imipramine, isocarboxazid, dextroamphetamine-amobarbital and placebo. *Clin. Pharmacol. Ther.* 3: 16–22.

(21) Greenblatt, M., Grosser, G.H., and Wechsler, H. (1964): Differential response of hospitalized depressed patients to somatic therapy. *Amer. J. Psychiat.* 120: 935–943.

(22) Tetreault, L.: Comparative evaluation of antidepressant properties of opipramol, imipramine and a placebo in neurotic depression. *Proc. IV World Cong. of Psych.*: 2027–2089.

(23) Heller, A., Zahourek, R., and Whittington, H.G. (1971): Effectiveness of antidepressant drugs: a triple-blind study comparing imipramine, desipramine, and placebo. *Amer. J. Psychiat.* 127: 1092–1095.

(24) Agnew, P.C., Baran, I.D., Klapman, H.J., Reid, F.T., Stern, J.J., and Slut-

ske, R.H. (1961): A clinical evaluation of four antidepressant drugs (Nardil, Tofranil, Marplan and Deprol). *Amer. J. Psychiat.* 118: 160–162.

(25) Raskin, A., Schulterbrandt, J.G., Reatig, N., and McKeon, J. (1970): Differential response to chlorpromazine, imipramine and placebo. A study of subgroups of hospitalized depressed patients. *Arch. Gen. Psychiat.* 23: 164–173.

(26) Karkalas, Y. and Lal, H. (1970): Imipramine pamoate in hospitalized depressives: a double-blind comparison with placebo. *Psychosomatics* 11: 107–111.

(27) Wilson, I.C., Alltop, L., and Riley, L. (1970): Tofranil in the treatment of post alcoholic depression. *Psychosomatics* 11: 488–494.

(28) Wittenborn, J.R., Plante, M., Burgess, F., and Maurer, H. (1962): A comparison of imipramine, electroconvulsive therapy and placebo in the treatment of depressions. *J. Nerv. Ment. Dis.* 135: 131–137.

(29) Weintraub, W. and Aronson, H. (1963): Clinical judgment in psychopharmacological research. *J. Neuropsychiat.* 5: 65–70.

(30) Seager, C.P. and Bird, R.L. (1962): Imipramine with electrical treatment in depression: a controlled trial. *J. Ment. Sci.* 108: 704–707.

(31) Ruble, P.E. (1961): Psychic energizers in neurologically debilitated patients. *J. Neuropsychiat.* 2 (Suppl.): S66–S68.

(32) Robin, A.A. and Langley, G.E. (1964): A controlled trial of imipramine. *Brit. J. Psychiat.* 110: 419–422.

(33) Robin, A.A. and Harris, J.A. (1962): A controlled comparison of imipramine and electroplexy. *J. Ment. Sci.* 108: 217–219.

(34) Rees, L., Brown, A.C., and Benaim, S. (1961): A controlled trial of imipramine (Tofranil) in the treatment of severe depressive states. *J. Ment. Sci.* 107: 552–559.

(35) Miller, A., Baker, E.F., Lewis, D., and Jones, A. (1960): Imipramine, a clinical evaluation in a variety of settings. I. A controlled study of chronic depressed states treated with antidepressive drugs. *Canad. Psychiat. Ass. J.* 5: 150–160.

(36) Mandell, A.J., Markham, C.H., Tallman, F.F., and Mandell, M.P. (1962): Motivation and ability to move. *Amer J. Psychiat.* 119: 544–549.

(37) Leyberg, J.T. and Denmark, J.C. (1959): The treatment of depressive states with imipramine hydrochloride (Tofranil). *J. Ment. Sci.* 105: 1123–1126.

(38) Lehmann, H.E., Cahn, C.H., and deVerteuil, R.L. (1958): The treatment of depressive conditions with imipramine (G-22, 355). *Canad. Psychiat. Ass. J.* 3: 155–164.

(39) Klein, D.F. (1966): Chlorpromazine-procyclidine combination, imipramine and placebo in depressive disorders. *Canad. Psychiat. Ass. J.* 11(Suppl.): 146–149.

(40) Kenning, I.S., Richardson, N.L., and Tucker, F.G. (1960): The treatment of depressive states with imipramine hydrochloride. *Canad. Psychiat. Ass. J.* 5: 60–64.

(41) Holdway, V. (1960): Trial imipramine. *J. Ment. Sci.* 106: 1443–1446.

(42) Greenblatt, M., Grosser, G.H., and Wechsler, H. (1964): Choice of somatic therapies in depression. *Curr. Psychiat. Ther.* 4: 134–142.

(43) Friedman, C., DeMowbray, M., and Hamilton, V. (1961): Imipramine (Tofranil) in depressive states. *J. Ment. Sci.* 107: 948–953.

(44) Daneman, E.A. (1961): Imipramine in office management of depressive reactions (a double-blind clinical study). *Dis. Nerv. Syst.* 22: 213–217.

(45) Desai, R.G., Shah, L.P., Bagadia, V.N., and Vahia, N.S. (1961): Value of imipramine (Tofranil) in depression (a preliminary report). *J. of J. J. Group of Hospitals and Grant Med. Coll.* (Bombay) 6: 101–108.

(46) Prange, A.J., Jr., McCurdy, R.L., and Cochrane, C.M. (1967): The systolic blood pressure response of depressed patients to norepinephrine. *J. Psychiat. Res.* 5: 1–13.

(47) Ashby, W.R. and Collins, G.H. (1961): A clinical trial of imipramine (Tofranil) on depressed patients. *J. Ment. Sci.* 107(488): 547–551.

(48) Fink, M., Pollack, M., Klein, D.F., Blumberg, A.G., Belmont, I., Karp, E., Kramer, J.C., and Willner, A. (1961): Comparative studies of chlorpromazine and imipramine. I. Drug discriminating patterns. In Bradley, P.B., Flugel, F., Hoch, P. (eds.) *Neuro-psychopharmacology.* 3: 370–372.

(49) Hohn, R., Gross, G.M., Gross, M., and Lasagna, L. (1961): A double-blind comparison of placebo and imipramine in the treatment of depressed patients in a state hospital. *J. Psychiat. Res.* 1: 76–91.

(50) Roulet, N., Alvarez, R.R., Duffy, J.P., Lenkoski, L.D., and Bidder, T.G. (1962): Imipramine in depression, a controlled study. *Amer. J. Psychiat.* 119: 427–431.

(51) Wilson, I.C., Vernon, J.T., and Sandifer, M.G., Jr. (1963): A controlled study of treatment of depression. *J. Neuropsychiat.* 4: 331–337.

(52) Fieve, R.R., Platman, S.R., and Plutchik, R.R. (1968): The use of lithium in affective disorders: 1. Acute endogenous depression. *Amer. J. Psychiat.* 112: 487–491.

(53) Lovett, J.W., Lewis, D.J., Sprott, D., and Wright, R.L. (1959): Controlled assessment of antidepressant drugs, including Tofranil. *Canad. Psychiat. Ass. J.* 4(Suppl.): S190–S194.

(54) DiFuria, G. and Marks, J.B. (1963): Methotrimeprazine as an adjunct to imipramine in depression. *Russ. Neuropsychiat.* 17: 210–219.

(55) Friedman, A.S., Granick, S., Cohen, H.W., and Cowitz, B. (1966): Imipramine (Tofranil) versus placebo in hospitalized psychotic depressives. *J. Psychiat. Res.* 4: 13–36.

(56) Fryer, D.G. and Timberlake, W.H. (1963): A trial of imipramine (Tofranil) in depressed patients with chronic physical disease. *J. Chronic Dis.* 16: 173–178.

(57) Sloane, R.B., Habib, A., and Batt, V.E. (1959): The use of imipramine (Tofranil) for depressive states in open ward settings of a general hospital. *Canad. Med. Ass. J.* 80: 540.

(58) Heimann, H., Hursch, L., Erseit, H.G., and Huber, H. (1969): Clinical and experimental demonstration of mood changes: double-blind tests with imipramine, ketoimipramine and placebo. *Arzn. Forsch.* 19: 467–469.

(59) Pokorny, A.D. and Overall, J.E. (1961): Preliminary report on V.A. cooperative study No. 5: chemotherapy of depression. 1. Background and description 2. Results. In *Transactions of the 6th Res. Conference on Cooperative Chemotherapy Studies in Psychiat. and Broad Res. Approaches to Mental Illness.* Washington V.A. Dept. of Med. and Surg. pp. 9–20.

(60) Rothman, T., Grayson, H., and Ferguson, J. (1961): A comparative investigation of isocarboxazid and imipramine in depressive syndromes, autonomic measures. *Proceedings 3rd World Congress of Psychiat.,* Montreal, pp. 937–941.

(61) Bellak, L. and Rosenberg, S. (1966): Effects of antidepressant drugs on psychodynamics. *Psychosomatics* 7: 106–114.

(62) Hollister, L.E., Overall, J.E., Johnson, M., Pennington, V., Katz, G., and Shelton, J. (1964): Controlled comparison of amitriptyline, imipramine, and placebo in hospitalized depressed patients. *J. Nerv. Ment. Dis.* 139: 370–375.

(63) Gallant, D.M., Bishop, M.P., Nesselhof, W., and Fulmer, T.E. (1964): JB–8181: antidepressant activity in outpatients. *Curr. Ther. Res.* 6: 69–70.

(64) Vestre, N.D., Janecek, J., and Zimmermann, R. (1967): A controlled study of desipramine in the treatment of hospitalized depressive disorders. *Int. J. Neuropsychiat.* 3: 354–359.

(65) Lapolla, A. and Jones, H. (1970): Placebo-control evaluation of desipramine in depression. *Amer. J. Psychiat.* 127: 335–338.

(66) Azima, H., Silver, A., and Arthurs, D. (1962): Effects of G33,040 (Ensidon) and G-35,020 (Pertofrane) on depressive states. *Canad. Med. Ass. J.* 87: 1224–1228.

(67) Downing, R.W. and Rickels, K. (1972): Predictors of amitriptyline response in outpatient depressives. *J. Nerv. Ment. Dis.* 154: 248–263.

(68) Marakinijo, V.O. (1970): Amitriptyline and chlordiazepoxide (Limbitrol) in depressive states in Nigerians. *Afri. J. Med. Sci.* 1–409–14.

(69) Rickels, K., Gordon, P.E., Jenkins, B.W., Perloff, M., Sachs, I., and Stepansky, W. (1970): Drug treatment in depressive illness: amitriptyline and chlorodiazepoxide in two neurotic populations. *Dis. Nerv. Syst.* 31: 30–42.

(70) Blashki, I.G., Mowbray, R., and Davis, B. (1971): Controlled trial of amitriptyline in general practice. *Brit. Med. J.* 1: 123–128.

(71) Master, R.S. (1963): Amitriptyline in depressive states, a controlled trial in India. *Brit. J. Psychiat.* 109: 826–829.

(72) Diamond, S. (1966): Double-blind controlled study of amitriptyline-perphenazine combination in medical office patients with depression and anxiety. *Psychosomatics* 7: 371–375.

(73) Rickels, K., Gordon, P.E., Weise, C.C., Bazilian, S.E., Feldman, H.S., and

Wilson, D.A. (1970): Amitriptyline and trimipramine in neurotic depressed outpatients: a collaborative study. *Amer. J. Psychiat.* 127: 208–218.

(74) Daneman, E.A. (1965): Clinical experience and a double-blind study of a new antidepressant, Vivactil hydrochloride. *Psychosomatics* 6: 342–346.

(75) Rickels, K., Hesbacher, P., and Downing, R.W. (1970): Differential drug effects in neurotic depression. *Dis. Nerv. Syst.* 31: 468–475.

(76) Inglis, J., Jones, R.P., and Sloane, R.B. (1963): A psychiatric and psychological study of amitriptyline (Elavil) as an antidepressant. *Canad. Med. Ass. J.* 88: 797–802.

(77) Brick, H., Doub, W., Jr., and Perdue, W.C. (1962): Effects of amitriptyline on depressive and anxiety states in penitentiary inmates. *Dis. Nerv. Syst.* 23: 572–574.

(78) Browne, M.W., Kreeger, L.C., and Kazamias, N.S. (1963): A clinical trial of amitriptyline in depressive patients. *Brit. J. Psychiat.* 109: 692–694.

(79) Garry, J. and Leonard, T.J. (1963): Trial of amitriptyline in chronic depression. *Brit. J. Psychiat.* 109: 54–55.

(80) Skarbek, A. and Smedberg, D. (1962): Amitriptyline: A controlled trial in chronic depressive states. *J. Ment. Sci.* 108: 859–861.

(81) Ekdawi, M.Y. (1971): Dibenzepin and amitriptyline in the treatment of depression. *Brit J. Psychiat.* 118(546): 523–524.

(82) McDonald, I.M., Perkins, M., and Marjerrison, G. (1966): A controlled comparison of amitriptyline and ECT in the treatment of depression. *Amer. J. Psychiat.* 122: 1427–1431.

(83) Taverna, P. and Ferrari, G. (1969): A comparison of nortriptyline, amitriptyline and placebo on the treatment of anxiety and depression. *Mineiva Medica.* 60: 2417–2431.

(84) Rees, L. and Davis, B. (1965): A controlled study of amitriptyline in severe depressed states. *Int. J. Neuropsychiat.* 1: 158–160.

(85) Hall, J. and Lonie, D. (1962): A controlled pilot trial of amitriptyline for treatment of depression in inpatients. *New Zeal. Med. J.* 61: 548–550.

(86) Davis, W.G. (1967): Treatment of anxiety and depression. A double-blind study of perphenazine and amitriptyline combination. *Rocky Mt. Med. J.* 64(11): 73–76.

(87) Quinones, J.A. (1967): Protriptyline hydrochloride in the ambulatory treatment of depressive conditions. *Rev. de Clin. Psic. Neur.* 4(2–3): 224–232.

(88) Chesrow, E.J., Kaplitz, S.E., Breme, J.T., Sabatini, R., Vetra, H., and Marguardt, G.H. (1964): Nortriptyline for the treatment of anxiety and depression in chronically ill and geriatric patients. *Amer. J. Geriat. Soc.* 12: 271–277.

(89) Nodine, J.H., Siegler, P.E., Bodi, T., Mapp, Y., and Dykyj, R. (1965): A variable dose phase 3, human bioassay of nortriptyline. *Amer. J. Med. Sci.* 250: 433–447.

(90) Barron, A., Rudy, L.H., and Smith, J.A. (1964): Clinical evaluation of a secondary amine, nortriptyline. *Amer. J. Psychiat.* 121: 268–269.

(91) Hays, P. and Steinert, J. (1969): A blind comparative trial of nortripty-line and isocarboxazid in depressed outpatients. *Canad. Psychiat. Ass. J.* 14: 307–308.

(92) Kozlowski, V.L., Williams, J.R., and Misevic, G. (1968): A study of the effects of Aventyl HCL (nortriptyline hydrochloride) in the treatment of patients with depressive symptoms. *Ill. Med. J.* 133: 161–165.

(93) Simeon, J., Spero, M., Nikolovski, O.T., et al. (1970): A comparison of doxepin and chlorodiazepoxide in the therapy of anxiety. *Curr. Ther. Res.* 12: 201–212.

(94) Fielding, J.M., Mowbray, R.M., and Davis, B. (1969): A preliminary controlled study of doxepin ("Sinequan") as an anti-anxiety drug. *Med. J. Ass.* 2: 851–852.

(95) Hutchinson, J.T. and Smedberg, D. (1963): Treatment of depression: a comparative study of ECT and six drugs. *Brit. J. Psychiat.* 109: 536–538.

(96) Akimoto, H., Kurihara, M., Fujiya, Y., Toyoda, J., and Sasaki, K. (1965): Differences in mode of action among so-called antidepressant drugs. In Bente, D. and Bradley, P.B. (eds.). *Neuropsychopharmacology: Proceedings of the 4th meeting of the Colleguim Internationale Neuro-psychopharmacologicum*, Sept. 1964. Amsterdam, Elsevier, pp. 421–427.

(97) Straker, M., Davonloo, H., and Moll, A. (1966): A double-blind comparison of a new antidepressant, protriptyline, with imipramine and amitriptyline. *Canad. Med. Ass. J.* 94: 1220–1222.

(98) Nahunek, K. (1970): Actual problems of endogenous and exogenous depressions. *Act. Nerv. Sup.* 12: 93–95.

(99) Snow, L.H. and Rickels, K. (1964): The controlled evaluation of imipramine and amitriptyline in hospitalized depressed psychiatric patients. A contribution to the methodology of drug evaluation. *Psychopharmacologia* 5: 409–416.

(100) Sandifer, M.G., Wilson, I.C., and Gambill, J.M. (1965): The influence of case selection and dosage in an antidepressant drug trial. *Brit. J. Psychiat.* 111: 142–148.

(101) Ravn, J. (1966): A comparison of past and present treatments of endogenous depression. *Brit. J. Psychiat.* 112: 501–504.

(102) Richmond, P.W. and Robert, A.H. (1964): A comparative trial of imipramine, amitriptyline, isocarboxazid and tranylcypromine in outpatient depressive illness. *Brit. J. Psychiat.* 110: 846–850.

(103) Weiss, L.B. and Pressman, M.D. (1961): A comparison of imipramine (Tofranil) and amitriptyline (Elavil) in the treatment of depression. *Psychosomatics* 2: 293–296.

(104) Mucha, H., Lange, E., and Bonitz, G. (1970): Amitriptyline in psychiatric therapy. *Psych. Neur. Med. Psych.* 22: 116–120.

(105) Hordern, A., Holt, N.F., Burt, C.G., and Gordon, W.F. (1963): Amitriptyline in depressive states: phenomenology and prognostic considerations. *Brit. J. Psychiat.* 109: 815–825.

(106) Hordern, A., Burt, C.G., and Holt, N.F. (1965): *Depressive States.* Charles C Thomas, Publisher, Springfield, 1965, pp. 40–49.

(107) *Ibid.*, pp. 109–116.

(108) Hoenig, J. and Visram, S. (1964): Amitriptyline versus imipramine in depressive psychoses. *Brit. J. Psychiat.* 110: 840–845.

(109) Burt, C.G., Gordon, W.F., Holt, N.F., and Hordern, A. (1962): Amitriptyline in depressive states: a controlled trial. *J. Ment. Sci.* 108: 711.

(110) Edwards, G. (1965): Comparison of the effect of imipramine and desipramine on some symptoms of depressive illness. *Brit. J. Psychiat.* 111: 889–97.

(111) LaFave, H.G., March, B.W., and Kargas, A.K. (1965): Desipramine and imipramine in an outpatient setting: a comparative study. *Amer. J. Psychiat.* 122: 698–701.

(112) Krakowski, A.J. (1967): New desipramine for treatment of depression. In Dunlop, E. and Weisman, M.N. (eds.). *Proceedings of the First International Academy of Psychosomatic Medicine, Excerpta Med. Found. Int. Congress Series.* 134: 5–10.

(113) Hargreaves, M.A. and Maxwell, C. (1967): The speed of action of desipramine: a controlled trial. *Int. J. Neuropsychiat.* 3: 140–141.

(114) Wilson, I.C., Gambell, J.M., and Sandifer, M.G., Jr. (1964): A double-blind study comparing imipramine (Tofranil) with desmethylimipramine (Pertofrane). *Psychosomatics* 5: 88.

(115) Waldron, J. and Bates, J.T.N. (1965): The management of depression in hospital. A comparative trial of desipramine and imipramine. *Brit. J. Psychiat.* 111: 511–516.

(116) St. Jean, A., Ban, T.A., and Noe, W. (1966): The effect of iminodibenzyls in the treatment of chronic psychotic patients. *Curr. Ther. Res.* 8: 164–165.

(117) Rose, J.T. and Westhead, T.T. (1967): Treatment of depression. A comparative trial of imipramine and desipramine. *Brit. J. Psychiat.* 113: 659–665.

(118) Rose, J.T. and Westhead, T.T. (1964): Comparison of desipramine and imipramine in depression. *Amer. J. Psychiat.* 121: 496–498.

(119) Agin, H.V., Greenblatt, I.J., and Agin, M.J. (1965): A double-blind study of desipramine (Norpramin) with imipramine (Tofranil) with clinical psychological observations and cross-overs. *Psychosomatics* 6: 320–321.

(120) Rose, J.T. and Maxwell, C. (1969): Depression: Prognosis and drug treatment. *Dis. Nerv. Syst.* 30: 186–188.

(121) Burns, B.H. (1965): Preliminary evaluation of a new antidepressant trimipramine, by a sequential method. *Brit. J. Psychiat.* 111: 1115–1157.

(122) Salzmann, M.M. (1965): A controlled trial with trimipramine, a new antidepressant drug. *Brit. J. Psychiat.* 111: 1105–1106.

(123) Kessell, A., Pearce, T.A., and Holt, N.F. (1970): A controlled study of nortriptyline and imipramine. *Amer. J. Psychiat.* 126: 938–945.

(124) Isaksson, A., Larkander, O., and Morsing, C. (1968): A comparison be-

tween imipramine and protriptyline in the treatment of depressed outpatients. *Acta Psychiat. Scand.* 44: 205–223.

(125) Périer, M. and Eslami, H. (1971): Clinical evaluation of the antidepressant effects of doxepine. *Annales Med. Psychol.* 1: 581–587.

(126) Hasan, K.Z. and Akhtar, M.I. (1971): Double-blind clinical study comparing doxepin and imipramine in depression. *Curr. Ther. Res.* 13: 327–336.

(127) Castrogiovanni, P., Placidi, G., Maggini, C., Ghetti, B., and Cassano, G. (1971): Clinical investigation of doxepin in depressed patients. Pilot open study, controlled double-blind trial versus imipramine and all-night polygraphic study. *Pharm. Neuro-psychopharm.* 4: 170–180.

(128) Forrest, A.D., Affleck, J.W., and Gibb, I.A. (1964): Comparative trial of nortriptyline and amitriptyline. *Scot. Med. J.* 9: 341–344.

(129) Mendels, J. (1968): Comparative trial of nortriptyline and amitriptyline in 100 depressed patients. *Amer. J. Psychiat.* 124(Suppl.): 59–62.

(130) Leahy, M.R. and Martin, I.C. (1967): Double-blind comparison of nortriptyline and amitriptyline in depressive illness. *Brit. J. Psychiat.* 113: 1433–1434.

(131) Rose, J.T., Leahy, M.R., and Martin, I.C. (1965): A comparison of nortriptyline and amitriptyline in depression. *Brit. J. Psychiat.* 111: 1101–1103.

(132) Martin, I.C. and Leahy, M.R. (1968): Prediction in antidepressant therapy. *Brit. J. Psychiat.* 114: 1289–1291.

(133) McConaghy, A. (1968): Correlation of clinical features with response to amitriptyline and protriptyline. *Brit. J. Psychiat.* 114: 103–106.

(134) McConaghy, N., Kingston, W.R., and Stevenson, H.G. (1965): A controlled trial comparing amitriptyline and protriptyline in the treatment of outpatient depressives. *Med. J. Aust.* 2: 403–405.

(135) Brick, H., Doub, W. H., Jr., and Perdue, W.C. (1965): A comparison of the effects of amitriptyline and protriptyline on anxiety and depressive states in female prisoners. *Int. J. Neuropsychiat.* 1: 325–336.

(136) Williams, E.J. (1968): A double-blind clinical trial. *Med. J. Aust.* 55: 537–540.

(137) Bianchi, G.N., Barr, R.F., and Kiloh, L.G. (1971): A comparative trial of doxepin and amitriptyline in depressive illness. *Med. J. Aust.* 1: 843–846.

(138) Hackett, E. and Kline, N.S. (1969): Antidepressant activity of doxepin and amitriptyline. A double-blind evaluation. *Psychosomatics* 10: 21–24.

(139) Bauer, G. and Nowak, H. (1969): Doxepin, a new antidepressant; comparison of activity with amitriptyline. *Arzn. Forsch.* 19: 1642–1646.

(140) Jones, B.L., Eastgate, N.O., Downey, P.G., and Davies, L.J.H. (1972): A comparison of doxepin with diazepam and amitriptyline in general practice. *N. Z. Med. J.* 76: 174–179.

(141) Gomez-Martinez, I. (1968): Preliminary double-blind clinical trial with a new antidepressive doxepin. *Curr. Ther. Res.* 10: 116–118.

(142) Toru, M., Takamizawa, M., Kariya, T., Kobayashi, K., and Takahashi, R. (1972): A double-blind sequential comparison of doxepin with amitriptyline in depressed patients. *Psychosomatics* 13: 241–250.

(143) Querol, M. (1970): A double-blind study with antidepressants. *Rev. Neuropsiquiat* 33: 251–270.

(144) Lipsedge, M.S. and Rees, W.L. (1971): A double-blind comparison of dothiepin and amitriptyline for the treatment of depression with anxiety. *Psychopharmacologia* 19: 153–162.

(145) Solis, H., Molina, G., and Piñeyro, A. (1970): Clinical evaluation of doxepin and amitriptyline in depressed patients. *Curr. Ther. Res.* 12: 524–527.

(146) Haider, I. (1968): A comparative investigation of desipramine and nortriptyline in the treatment of depression. *Brit. J. Psychiat.* 114: 1293–1294.

(147) Stewart, J.A. and Mitchell, P.H. (1968): A comparative trial of desipramine and nortriptyline in depression. *Brit. J. Psychiat.* 114: 469–471.

(148) Arbitman, R., Yurtcu, A., Lehmann, H.E., Sterlin, C., Ban, T.A., and Jarrold, L. (1970): Protriptyline in the treatment of chronic schizophrenic patients. *Curr. Ther. Res.* 12: 131–135.

(149) Splitter, S.R. (1963): Comprehensive treatment of office patients with the aid of a new psychophysiologic agent opipramol (Ensidon). *Psychosomatics* 4: 283–289.

(150) Shepherd, F.S. (1965): A study of opipramol in general practice. *Practitioner* 195: 92–95.

(151) Weckowicz, T.E. (1967): A clinical trial of G-33040 in a group of depressed outpatients. *Canad. Psychiat. Ass. J.* 12: 603–606.

(152) Carney, M.W.P. (1968): Investigations of the clinical effects of opipramol. *Proceedings of the 4th World Congress of Psychiatry.* 3: 1904–1908.

(153) Rajotte, P., Bordeleau, J.M., and Tetreault, L. (1966): A double blind comparative study of opipramol and amitriptyline in neurotic and endogenous depressions. *Canad. Psychiat. Ass. J.* 11: 159–168.

(154) Gayral, L., Puyuolo, R., and Rouv, G. (1964): Observations on the actions of trimipramine in comparison to the effect of a placebo. *Therapie.* 20: 639–654.

(155) Burke, B.V., Sainsbury, M.J., and Mezo, B.A. (1967): A comparative trial of amitriptyline and trimipramine in the treatment of depression. *Med. J. Aust.* 1: 1216–1218.

(156) Kristof, F.E., Lehmann, H.E., and Ban, T.A. (1967): Systematic studies with trimipramine: a new antidepressive drug. *Canad. Psychiat. Ass. J.* 12: 517–520.

(157) Kristof, F.E., Lehmann, H.E., and Ban, T.A. (1968): Trimipramine for depression. *Appl. Ther.* 10: 470.

(158) Daneman, E.A. (1967): Treatment of depressed patients with iprindole. *Psychosomatics* 8: 216–221.

(159) Hicks, J.T. (1965): Iprindole, a new antidepressant for use in general office practice. A double-blind, placebo-controlled study. *Ill. Med. J.* 128: 622–626.

(160) Rickels, K., Gordon, P.E., Meckelnburg, R., Sablosky, L., Whalen, E.M., and Dion, H. (1968): Iprindole in neurotic depressed general practice patients: a controlled study. *Psychosomatics* 9: 208–214.

(161) Hankoff, L.D., Heller, B., and Galvin, J.W. (1962): The setting in psychopharmacological treatment: outpatient usage of antidepressants. *Psychosomatics* 3: 201–208.

(162) Kurland, A.A., Destounis, N., Shaffer, J.W., and Pinto, A. (1967): A critical study of isocarboxazid (Marplan) in the treatment of depressed patients. *J. Nerv. Ment. Dis.* 145: 292–305.

(163) Ford, R.B., Branham, H.E., and Cleckly, J.J. (1959): Isocarboxazid: a new antidepressant drug. *Clin. Med.* 6: 1559–1561.

(164) Feldstein, A., Hoagland, H., Rivera, O.M., and Freeman, H. (1965): MAO inhibition and antidepressant activity. *Int. J. Neuropsychiat.* 1: 384–387.

(165) Dewhurst, W.G. (1968): Methysergide in mania. *Nature* 219: 506–507.

(166) Rickels, K., Ward, C., and Snow, L. (1963): Nialamide and placebo in depressed psychiatric clinic patients. (A controlled double-blind study). *Dis. Nerv. Syst.* 24: 548–550.

(167) Shah, L.P., Shah, V.D., and Bagadia, V.N. (1964): Value and limitations of nialamide in depression. *Indian J. Med. Sci.* 18: 643–647.

(168) Inglis, J., Caird, W.K., and Sloane, R.B. (1961): An objective assessment of the effects of nialamide on depressed patients. *Canad. Med. Ass. J.* 84: 1059.

(169) Nussbaum, K., Wittig, B.A., and Hanlon, T.E. (1963): Intravenous nialamide in the treatment of depressed female patients. *Compr. Psychiat.* 4: 105–116.

(170) Oltman, J.E. and Friedman, S. (1963): Pargyline in the treatment of depressive illnesses. *Amer. J. Psychiat.* 120: 493–494.

(171) Jacobs, M.A. and Pillard, R. (1965): Approach to studying drug effects in ambulatory patients. *Arch. Gen. Psychiat.* 13: 163–171.

(172) Glick, B.S. (1964): Double-blind study of tranylcypromine and phenelzine in depression. *Dis. Nerv. Syst.* 25: 617–619.

(173) Bartholomew, A.A. (1962): An evaluation of tranylcypromine (Parnate) in the treatment of depression. *Med. J. Aust.* 49: 655–662.

(174) Kharna, J.L., Pratt, S., and Burdizk, E.G. (1963): A study of certain effects of tranylcypromine, a new antidepressant. *J. New Drugs* 3: 227–232.

(175) Gottfries, C.G. (1963): Clinical trial with the monoamine oxidase inhibitor tranylcypromine on a psychiatric clientele. *Acta Psychiat. Scand.* 39: 463–472.

(176) Hare, E.H., Dominian, J., and Sharpe, L. (1962): Phenelzine and dexamphetamine in depressive illness. A comparative trial. *Brit. Med. J.* 1: 9–12.

(177) Hutchinson, J.T. and Smedberg, D. (1960): Phenelzine (Nardil) in the treatment of endogenous depression. *J. Ment. Sci.* 106: 704–710.

(178) Rees, L. and Davies, B. (1961): A controlled trial of phenelzine (Nardil) in the treatment of severe depressive illness. *J. Ment. Sci.* 107: 560–570.

(179) Middlefell, R., Frost, I., Egan, G.P., and Eaton, H. (1960): A report on the effects of phenelzine (Nardil), a monoamine oxidase inhibitor, in depressed patients. *J. Ment. Sci.* 106: 1533–1538.

(180) Haydu, G.G., Whittier, J.R., and Goldschmidt, L. (1964): Differential therapeutic results of three antidepressant medications according to fixed or functional schedules. *J. Nerv. Ment. Dis.* 139: 475–478.

(181) Martin, M.E. (1963): A comparative trial of imipramine and phenelzine in the treatment of depression. *Brit. J. Psychiat.* 109: 279–285.

(182) Ayd, F.J., Jr. (1960): Antidepressant, 1959. *Psychosomatics* 1: 37–41.

(183) Ainslie, J.D., Steifel, J.R., and Jones, M.B. (1966): Practical drug evaluation method. II. A drug-drug comparison. *Arch. Gen. Psychiat.* 15: 368–372.

(184) Oltman, J.E. and Friedman, S. (1961): Comparison of Marplan and Tofranil in the treatment of depressive states. *Amer. J. Psychiat.* 117: 929–930.

(185) Sheard, M.H. (1963): The influence of doctor's attitude on the patient's response to antidepressant medication. *J. Nerv. Ment. Dis.* 136: 555–560.

(186) Leith, A. and Seager, C.P. (1963): A trial of four antidepressant drugs. *Psychopharmacologia* 4: 72–77.

(187) Imlah, N.W., Fahy, P.T., and Harrington, J.A. (1964): A comparison of two antidepressant drugs. *Psychopharmacologia* 6: 472–474.

(188) O'Reilly, P.O. and Hughes, E. (1961): Efficacy of antidepressants. *Canad. Med. Ass. J.* 84: 887–888.

(189) Haydu, G.G., Brinitzer, W., McKnight, J.N., and Whittier, J.R. (1961): A comparative trial of antidepressants. *Dis. Nerv. Syst.* 22(Suppl. 4): 90–92.

(190) Leuthold, C.A., Bradshaw, F.J., Jr., Arndt, G.W., Hoffman, E.F., and Pishkin, V. (1961): Behavioral evaluation of imipramine and nialamide in regressed schizophrenic patients with depressive features. *Amer. J. Psychiat.* 118: 354–355.

(191) Akimoto, H., Nakakuki, M., and Machiyama, Y. (1960): Clinical experiences with MAO inhibitors: a comparison with Tofranil. *Dis. Nerv. Syst.* 21: 645–648.

(192) Spear, F.G., Hall, P., and Stirland, J.D. (1964): A comparison of subjective responses to imipramine and tranylcypromine. *Brit. J. Psychiat.* 110: 53–54.

(193) Bruce, E.M., Crone, N. Fitzpatrick, G., Frewin, S.J., Gillis, A., Lascelles, C.F., Levene, L.J., and Merskey, H. (1960): A comparative trial of ECT and Tofranil. *Amer. J. Psychiat.* 117: 76.

(194) Greenblatt, M., Grosser, G.H., and Wechsler, H. (1962): A comparative study of selected antidepressant medications and ECT. *Amer. J. Psychiat.* 119: 144–153.

(195) Fahy, P., Imlah, N., and Harrington, J. (1963): A controlled comparison of electroconvulsive therapy, imipramine and thiopentone sleep in depression. *J. Neuropsychiat*, 4: 310–314.

(196) Stanely, W.J. and Fleming, H. (1962): A clinical comparison of phenelzine and ECT in the treatment of depressive illness. *J. Ment. Sci.* 108: 708–710.

(197) King, P.D. (1959): Phenelzine and ECT in the treatment of depression. *Amer. J. Psychiat.* 116: 64–68.

(198) Hansen, C.J., Retboll, K., and Schou, M. cited by Schou, M. (1959): Lithium in psychiatric therapy. Stock taking after ten years. *Psychopharmacologia* 1: 65–78.

(199) Goodwin, F.K., Murphy, D.L., and Bunney, W.E., Jr. (1969): Lithium carbonate treatment in depression and mania: a longitudinal double-blind behavioral and biochemical study. *Arch. Gen. Psychiat.* 21: 486–496.

(200) Platman, S.R. (1970): Comparison of lithium carbonate and imipramine (in prevention of manic depressive disease). *Dis. Nerv. Syst.* 31: 132–134.

(201) Mendels, J., Secunda, S.K., and Dyson, L. (1972): A controlled study of the antidepressant effects of lithium carbonate. *Arch. Gen. Psychiat.* 26: 154–157.

(202) Coppen, A., Noguera, R., Bailey, J., Burns, B.H., Swani, M.S., Hare, E.H., Gardner, R., and Maggs, R. (1971): Prophylactic lithium in affective disorders. Controlled trial. *Lancet* 2: 275–279.

(203) Schou, M. (1971): Lithium prophylaxis in manic-depressive psychosis and in recurrent endogenous depressions. *Nerv. Psychiat.* 10: 217–224.

(204) Angst, J., Weis, P., Grof, P., Baastrup, P.C., and Schou, M. (1970): Lithium prophylaxis in recurrent affective disorders. *Brit. J. Psychiat.* 116: 604–614.

(205) Polackova, J., Bily, J., and Hanus, H. (1971): Results of lithium treatment of manic-depressive psychosis in comparison with the control group. *Act. Nerv. Sup.* 13: 171.

(206) Melia, P.I. (1970): Prophylactic lithium: a double-blind trial in recurrent affective disorders. *Brit. J. Psychiat.* 116: 621–624.

(207) Fieve, R.R., Platman, S.R., and Plutchik, R.R. (1968): The use of lithium in affective disorders: II Prophylaxis of depression in chronic recurrent affective disorder. *Amer. J. Psychiat.* 125: 492–498.

(208) Busfield, B., Jr., Schneller, P., and Capra, D. (1962): Depressive symptom or side effect? A comparative study of symptoms during pre-treatment and treatment periods of patients on three anti-depressant medications. *J. Nerv. Ment. Dis.* 134: 339–345.

(209) Bird, C.E. (1960): Agranulocytosis due to imipramine (Tofranil). *Canad. Med. Assn. J.* 82: 1021–1022.

(210) Curron, T.P. and Barabas, E. (1961): Agranulocytosis after imipramine and meprobramate. *Brit. Med. J.* 1: 257.

(211) Cohen, S.I. (1960): Agranulocytosis associated with imipramine. *Lancet.* 2: 1164.

(212) Goodman, H.L. (1961): Agranulocytosis associated with Tofranil. *Ann. Intern Med.* 55: 321–323.

(213) Rothenberg, P.A. and Hall, C. (1960): Agranulocytosis following use of imipramine hydrochloride (Tofranil). *Amer. J. Psychiat.* 116: 847.

(214) Hegardt, K. (1960): Agranulocytosis in imipramine therapy. *Svenska Lakartidn.* 57: 2073–2076.

(215) Honigfeld, G. and Newhall, P.N. (1964): Hemodynamic effects of aceto-phenazine imipramine and trifluoperazine in geriatric psychiatry. *Report No. 61, V.A. Central Neuropsychiatric Research Laboratory,* Perry Point, Maryland.

(216) Muller, O.F., Goodman, N., and Bellet, S. (1961): The hypotensive effect of imipramine hydrochloride in patients with cardiovascular disease. *Clin. Pharmacol. Ther.* 2: 300–307.

(217) Khun, R. (1958): The treatment of depressive states with G-22355 (imipramine hydrochloride). *Amer. J. Psychiat.* 115: 459–464.

(218) Mann, A.M. and MacPherson, A.S. (1959): Clinical experience with imi-pramine (G-22355) in the treatment of depression: further clinical expe-rience. *Canad. Med. Ass. J.* 88: 1102–1107.

(219) Sloman, L. (1960): Myocardial infarction during imipramine treatment of depression. *Canad. Assn. J. Med.* 28: 20.

(220) Lehmann, H.E., Cahn, C.H., and deVertevil, R.L. (1958): The treatment of depressive conditions with imipramine (G-22355). *Canad. Psychiat. Assn. J.* 3: 155–164.

(221) Freyhan, F.A., (1960): The modern treatment of depressive disorders. *Amer. J. Psychiat.* 116: 1057–1064.

(222) Sarwer-Foner, G.J., Graver, H., Mackay, J., and Koranyi, E.K. (1959): Depressive states and drugs. A study of the use of imipramine "Tofranil" in open psychiatric settings. *Canad. Med. Serv. J.* 15: 359–382.

(223) Shatan, C. (1966): Withdrawal symptoms after abrupt termination of imipramine. *Canad. Psychiat. Assn. J.* 11(Suppl.): 5150–5158.

(224) Editorial (1968): Tricyclic antidepressants. *Brit. Med. J.* 5597: 102–104.

(225) Asatoor, A.M., Levi, J.A., and Milne, M.D. (1963): Tranylcypromine and cheese. *Lancet* 2: 733–734.

(226) Kline, N.S. (1969): *Depression: Its Diagnosis and Treatment.* New York, Bruner/Mazel.

(227) Beck, A.T., Ward, C.H., Mendelson, M., Mock, J., and Erbaugh, J. (1961): An inventory for measuring depression. *Arch. Gen. Psychiat.* 4: 561–571.

(228) Zung, W.W.K. (1965): A self-rating depression scale. *Arch. Gen. Psychiat.* 12: 63–70.

(229) Paskind, H.A. (1929): Brief attacks of manic-depressive depression. *Arch. Neural. Psychiat.* 22: 123–134.

(230) Mendels, J. (1965): Electroconvulsive therapy and depression. *Brit. J. Psychiat.* 3: 675–681.

(231) Rickels, K.R., Gordon, P.E., Gansman, P.H., Weise, C.C., Pereira-Ogan, J.A., and Hesbacher, P.T. (1970): Pemoline and methylphenidate in mildly depressed outpatients. *Clinical Pharm. Therapeut.* 5: 698–710.

(232) Luborsky, L.L. (1972): Comparative studies of psychotherapies. (In press).

Chapter 7.
Electroconvulsive Therapy

Convulsions induced by substantial doses of camphor were used in the treatment of mental disorders as long ago as 1785. The treatment was revived in 1933 by Meduna who used camphor in the treatment of schizophrenic patients. Camphor was gradually replaced by more effective drugs such as Metrazol. In 1938, Cerletti and Bini refined the technique of producing convulsions when they introduced the technique of passing an electric current through two electrodes placed on the forehead. Consequently, a relatively safe, convenient, and painless method of convulsive therapy could be used in the treatment of mental disorders. Electroconvulsive therapy (ECT) was introduced into the United States by Kalinowski in 1939.

Although Metrazol is still used at several psychiatric centers for purposes of convulsive therapy, the most common method of producing therapeutic convulsions is at present electroshock.

PHYSIOLOGICAL EFFECTS

The physiological effects of ECT have been summarized by Holmberg (1963). Electroconvulsive therapy, when not modified by muscle relaxing agents, produces a grand mal seizure. Initially there is a tension or jerk produced by direct cortical stimulation. This is followed by a latent period and then by tonic and clonic convulsions. The electroencephalogram during the tonic phase is characterized by a generalized, intensive spike activity. During the clonic phase the EEG shows spike-wave activity that is not synchronous with the clonic movements. Immediately following the convulsion, the EEG shows a brief period of electrical silence followed by a gradual return of activity until the preconvulsive pattern is resumed.

Holmberg lists a variety of physiological changes that occur during the convulsion. Respiration is suspended as a result of spasm of the respiratory muscles and glottis. There is an elevation of the blood carbon dioxide tension and a substantial reduction of the oxygen tension. Although the cerebral circulation is markedly increased during the convulsion, the increased blood supply does not meet the demand of the tremendously increased brain metabolism. According to Holmberg, the discrepancy between the available cerebral circulation and the increased brain metabolism is the main reason for the spontaneous termination of the convulsion.

Anoxia is readily counteracted by the insufflation of oxygen prior to ECT. The heart rate is frequently rapid and irregular and there may be extreme fluctuations in blood pressure. The irregularity of the heart rate may be neutralized by premedication with atropine. Muscle relaxants may be used to reduce the increase in arterial pressure.

The immediate effects on the EEG following ECT are brief and reversible. The effects tend to be cumulative, however, over a series of treatments. They do not persist in general for more than a month following a course of treatment.

Some authors report a relationship between the degree of slowing of the EEG and clinical improvements. Others, however, deny the existence of such relationship.

Some investigators have reported an association between the severity of memory defects and the degree of EEG change. In other studies, however, no such correlation has been found. In general, the EEG changes are correlated more highly with memory defects than with the antidepressive effects.

ECT produces a variety of autonomic changes that are attributable to the excitation of the autonomic regulatory centers. One of the most prominent effects is psychomotor restlessness. A number of cholinergic effects such as transient arrhythmias may occur but these are easily controlled by the use of anticholinergic drugs. The increase in salivary and bronchial secretions may similarly be counteracted by preliminary atropinization.

BIOCHEMICAL EFFECTS

Holmberg discusses a number of biochemical and hormonal changes that have been reported in conjunction with ECT. Hyperglycemia of one to several hours duration is a constant phenomenon. There is also an increase in nitrogen compounds, potassium, calcium, phosphorus, and steroids in the blood. Several investigators have demonstrated an increase in the catecholamines and serotonin of the blood, but there is no evidence that this effect has anything to do with the therapeutic action of ECT.

Holmberg also lists certain specific biochemical changes within the brain. The serotonin level in the brain, and especially in the brain stem, is increased but there is no change in the brain amine oxidase activity. The increase in serotonin is attributed to the electrical stimulus and does not appear to be related to the intensity of the convulsion.

PSYCHOLOGICAL EFFECTS

Some impairment of memory occurs almost constantly with ECT. This impairment may range from a mild tendency to forget names or dates to a severe confusion. The amnesia may be both anterograde and retrograde. It is often disturbing to the patient and may continue for several weeks following the conclusion of treatment. The impairment of memory usually disappears within a month (Cronholm and Molander, 1964). There is no lasting impairment of memory even after as many as 250 treatments. Most authors believe that the efficacy of ECT in depression bears no relationship to the memory defects.

Holmberg suggests that very intensive treatment in elderly arteriosclerotic subjects may cause irreversible brain damage with resultant intellectual impairment. Others writers, however, do not believe that such a risk exists.

CLINICAL EFFICACY

Clinicians generally consider that the number of treatments necessary to clear a depression varies from 2–10. Frequently only four or five treatments are required and occasionally dramatic improvement is noted after only one treatment. There is some variability in the frequency of treatment, which may take place one to five times a week. Daily treatment may result in a cumulative confusion wheras treatments that are too widely spaced may increase the possibility of relapse.

Articles on the efficacy of ECT have reported improvement rates from 40 per cent to 100 per cent of patients in depressed states. Manic states are said to have a somewhat lower rate of response. The differences in results may be primarily due to differences of samples, but also may be influenced by variations in methods for assessing recovery. As has been observed in Chapter 3, depressed patients in the normal course of their illness show a very high percentage of spontaneous recovery. This varies from a median of 3–4 months among outpatients to a median of 6–18 months among inpatients. Despite the known tendency for spontaneous remission, the various psychiatric textbooks and the monographs on depression assert that ECT accelerates the improvement. On the other hand, manic-depressive patients who have received ECT seem to have a higher probability of recurrence and a shorter free interval period between attacks than patients who had a remission without receiving shock (Salzman, 1947).

Huston and Locher (1948) reported a recovery rate of 88 per cent in 74 manic-depressive patients who received ECT as compared with 79 per cent recovery rate for 63 patients who had been hospitalized before the introduction of ECT. The duration of illness was substantially less in the treated group (9 months vs. 15 months). Bond and Morris (1954) also compared patients hospitalized after the introduction of ECT with patients who were treated before the introduction of ECT. They found that the recovery rate for manic depressives was 72 per cent for the ECT group as compared with 59 per cent for the pre-ECT group. However, in those cases where 5-year follow-up studies could be completed, the differences were largely wiped out; the permanent recovery figures were 66 per cent for the patients of the current era and 64.5 per cent for the pre-ECT patients. One of the most conspicuous findings was the difference in the duration of hospitalization: 2.3 months for those admitted in the years after the introduction of ECT as compared with 4.5 months for patients admitted in the earlier period. The results with involutionals were much more dramatic. The five-year recovery rate of the treated cases was 56 per cent as compared with 27 per cent for the controls. The duration of hospitalization was 2 months and 12 months respectively.

There are a number of methodological difficulties in studies of this nature. One of the most common is that in follow-up it is easier to find records of patients who have relapsed than of those who have not. It is possible, also, that the more careful follow-up available with the later cases may have spuriously inflated the ratio of recurrences. Furthermore, there is no evidence that the samples taken at different eras were similar, or that other therapeutic factors, such as milieu therapy, were equivalent.

The more recent controlled studies have compared improvement rates of patients assigned randomly to ECT and a control group. Riddell (1963), in a review of the effectiveness of ECT, was able to locate only three controlled studies of this nature. In one, ECT was significantly more effective than no treatment; in the second, ECT was significantly more effective than a placebo; in the third, ECT was significantly more effective than iproniazid although the ECT relapse rate may have been higher.

In his review of antidepressant drugs, Davis (1965) found six studies comparing ECT with imipramine. Three studies showed no significant differences in their effectiveness but three showed ECT to be superior. Lumping together Riddell's and Davis' reviews, we can conclude that ECT was superior to no treatment or placebo in two studies; it was more effective than antidepressant drugs in four studies; and it was equivalent to drug therapy in three studies.

Although there is not very extensive evidence, it is widely believed that ECT is effective in the treatment of psychotic depression. All the reviewers of the drug studies who mention ECT say that no drug has been shown to be superior to it. [However, Cole (1964) and Hordern (1965) do not believe that ECT is effective or advisable for neurotic depressions.] Hordern, Cole, Davis, Klerman, and Cole (1965) and Wechsler, Grosser, and Greenblatt (1965), assert that the available reports indicate that ECT is superior to, or at least equal to, any drug treatment for psychotic depressives.

Whether drugs or ECT should be used in practice has been the subject of many polemics. The two sides of the argument are summarized by Hordern (1965). Disagreement also exists on whether ECT produces improvement *more rapidly* than any drug (Cole, 1964) and is therefore preferable in the treatment of severe depressions, particularly those with a danger of suicide.

A number of investigators have attempted to determine whether there are any *types* of depression, or configurations of clinical factors, that are predictive of a favorable outcome with ECT. In general, the studies of this nature (Carney, Roth, and Garside, 1965; and Mendels, 1965) have found favorable prognostic signs among the clinical features generally associated with so-called endogenous depression.

COMPLICATIONS

The most frequent complications are fractures and dislocations produced by the muscular contractions during the convulsions. The most frequent fracture is a compression fracture of the dorsal vertebrae. These fractures are generally not of major clinical significance and generally do not require special treatment; in fact, many are observed only on routine x-ray examination. Back pain may persist for a few days or weeks.

Fractures can be eliminated by *softening procedures*, viz., the use of muscle–relaxing agents. With well-modified ECT the strain on any part of the locomotor system can be reduced or eliminated.

At the present time, the only really important risks are cardiovascular accidents. Cardiovascular accidents are most likely to occur if there is preexisting pathology. Transient cardiac arrhythmias may occur but their incidence may be reduced by premedication with acetycholine-blocking agents. Succinylcholine greatly reduces the strain on the heart.

In earlier studies, the mortality risk for a specific patient was approximately 3 in 1,000. With the more modern modifications of ECT, the fatality rate is reduced even more. Holmberg reports that of several thousand electroconvulsive treatments that he has administered with pentobarbital-succinylcholine relaxation over a 10-year period there have been no complications.

MECHANISM OF ACTION

Kalinowsky and Hoch (1961) describe a wide variety of theories of the mode of action of ECT. While the mechanism of action has still not been established, it has been possible to eliminate many factors previously considered to be of major importance in producing therapeutic effects. Among the factors that can be discarded as therapeutically important are anoxia, hypercapnia, muscular exertion, adrenal reactions, peripheral excretion of catecholamines, and other biochemical changes in the blood (Holmberg).

Changes in the central nervous system, as manifested by the slowing of the EEG and intellectual impairment, are frequently claimed to have been responsible for the therapeutic improvement with ECT; however, proof is lacking to substantiate these claims.

The effectiveness of ECT is dependent on the production of seizure activity in the brain. Subconvulsive treatment and nonconvulsive electrostimulation of the diencephalon have been shown to be of no therapeutic value. Moreover, it has been reported that reducing the convulsive activity by premedication with anticonvulsive drugs reduces the therapeutic effect of ECT. On the other hand, intensification of the convulsive activity by the use of muscle relaxants and oxygenation increases the therapeutic effects (Holmberg).

Chapter 8.
Psychotherapy

REVIEW OF LITERATURE

In his book, *Manic-Depressive Disease*, Campbell (1953) suggests the following steps in the psychologic therapy of manic depressives:

First Step—Proper Diagnosis: An explicit diagnosis should be made and positive treatment begun. The physician cannot reassure his patient if he is not convinced himself. In the absence of positive physical or laboratory findings and the presence of sufficient autonomic disturbance, there is "no diagnosis in medicine as dependable as that of manic-depressive psychosis."

Second Step—Explanation of Somatic Symptoms: The physician should give the patient a physiologic explanation of his somatic symptoms. This knowledge and reassurance is helpful in obtaining the patient's cooperation and in achieving his relaxation.

Third Step—Removal of Precipitating or Aggravating Environmental Factors: The physician must be aware of the detailed history and of any provoking circumstances in the patient's life. It may be necessary to interview those close to the patient to ascertain what disturbing situations in the environment may be blocking his efforts to rest and relax.

Fourth Step—Combat Conscientiousness: The physician should make the patient aware that his inordinate conscientiousness stems from inner feelings of guilt, from an over-strict conscience, and from keen feelings of insecurity, and should encourage him to expect less of himself, to dispossess himself of the drive for accomplishment, and to develop a more nonchalant outlook on life. These changes, which may be achieved by insight, logic, and reasoning, may not only help to relieve the present illness, but may prevent future depressive reactions.

Fifth Step—Psychotherapy: In addition to reeducation, reassurance, and explanation, Campbell recommends simply allowing the patient to talk. The physician can also explain that this illness is self-limiting and that the patient will get well.

Sixth Step—Advice to the Family and Friends: The family should be told that the "patient has a well-recognized disease which happens to manifest itself by depression, indecision, crying spells, etc." It should be explained to them that this illness requires rest and relaxation, and that the patient must avoid anything that increases his tension and anxiety.

Seventh Step–Rest and Relaxation: The objective of the preceding six steps is to prepare the patient to rest, to relax, and to allow his nervous system a respite. The patient must be trained to relax and to realize the importance of rest to his hypersensitive nervous system, since work seems to be a compulsive phenomenon with the manic depressive.

Eighth Step–Occupational Therapy: Making or doing things with one's hands relieves anxiety, stimulates initiative and imagination, and produces a feeling of satisfaction. It is best if the patient discovers an avocation for himself rather than that the doctor assign one.

Ninth Step–Bibliotherapy: The patient should be encouraged to read to relax or to divert himself, rather than to improve his mind or personality; Campbell finds that there is not much benefit to be expected from the reading of books of an inspirational, religious nature.

In an article on the dynamics and psychotherapy of depression, Wilson (1955) points out that when the necessary state of personality equilibrium is disrupted, a "need-satisfaction sequence" is set up. Interruption of the need-satisfaction sequence produces anxiety. Turning on the self is a common substitute activity if the anxiety state cannot be satisfied by the actual object sought. The turning on the self produces a temporary or prolonged depression. Those people prone to an exaggerated depression show a special need as children for the approval of others. When young, they develop a technique by means of which they can obtain approval rather than developing a sense of self-worth or self-esteem. When the technique fails, the patient turns on himself, and becomes depressed.

Wilson recommends the following steps: (1) the therapist should show acceptance of the patient in spite of the patient's rejection of the therapist; (2) the patient should be shown how he continually seeks approval, how this has failed, and how he has turned on the self; (3) the therapist should show the patient how to be honest and direct; and (4) the therapist should support the patient in using more direct methods of self-expression.

Kraines, in his book *Mental Depressions and Their Treatment* (1957), stresses, as does Campbell, the physical basis of manic-depressive illness but considers psychotherapy essential to shorten the illness, to alleviate the patient's suffering, and to prevent complications. The therapy should be individualized according to the patient and to the phase of his illness and it may include medication, psychotherapy, direct guidance, and physical hygiene measures. Unlike Campbell, who feels that rest and relaxation are the major goals and who suggests curtailing of social contacts, Kraines believes that social activity should be encouraged. Both agree that in mild cases the patient does best when in his usual surroundings and both suggest institutional care and electric shock treatments when there is extreme agitation. Kraines and Campbell both stress "formulation to the patient," i.e. explaining to him the nature of his illness, emphasizing that he will be cured, and reassuring him that his illness has a physical basis. Both advise that relatives be informed that the patient is really ill despite the absence of objective medical tests.

The psychotherapy includes: (1) the *basic triad,*—understanding, hope, and plan; (2) utilization of the physician's personality (Success depends not only on technical knowledge but on the ability to establish rapport.); (3) the four levels of psychotherapy—ventilation, symptom management, mental hygiene principles, and deep personality analysis; and (4) therapeutic guidance. (Direct advice can be of great value but must be used with discretion according to individual needs.)

Ayd, in his book *Recognizing the Depressed Patient* (1961), also stresses (as do Campbell and Kraines) that the physician start by telling the patient that his illness has a physical basis and that he will improve. He feels that encouragement is important and that the physician should dissuade the patient from trying what is likely to be difficult since failure only reinforces his sense of inadequacy and guilt. Ayd feels that "no advantage is gained by an intellectual understanding of the psychological aspects of the illness," although he notes that it is important that the precipitating factors be analyzed and eliminated if possible so that the patient can be prepared to cope with similar problems in the future. Ayd states that many physicians do not seem to take cognizance of the natural course and duration of a depression and become discouraged when the response is slow or the patient retrogresses. He suggests that the physician involve family and friends in assisting and cooperating in the treatment of the depressed patient. He believes that informed relatives can assist the melancholic to carry out the doctor's instructions, can help to make environmental changes, and can fortify his desire to recover.

Ayd says it is essential that the depressed person obtain rest and relaxation which can only be achieved by changing his attitudes and habits since the depressive, goaded on by self-imposed standards and incited by feelings of guilt, tends to deny his feelings of fatigue and nervousness.

Arieti (1962) states that "Depression is . . . a reaction to the loss of a normal ingredient of psychological life." The patient must reorganize his thinking "into different constellations which do not bring about sadness." Depression changes the thought processes, apparently to decrease the quantity of thoughts "in order to decrease the quantity of suffering."

Arieti distinguishes between a "claiming depression" and a "self-blaming depression." In a claiming depression the patient is dependent on a dominant other and becomes more demanding as he feels more deprived. The self-blaming depression is an attempt to retrieve loss of the relationship to the dominant other by expiation. The mechanism's pattern is guilt, atoning, attempted redemption.

In cases of moderate intensity, Arieti suggests that the therapist alter the environment, especially the relationship to the dominant other; relieve the patient's feelings of guilt, responsibility, unaccomplishment, and loss; and disallow depressive thoughts to expand into general mood of depression.

Gibson (1963) in an article on psychotherapy of manic-depressive states, singles out two technical difficulties in the psychotherapy of manic depressives. The therapist should recognize the patient's difficulty in establishing a relationship with the therapist in which meaningful communication can take place. The patient tends to recast the therapist's remarks and interpretations into his own predetermined way of perceiving relationships. This "constellation" can be expected to reappear again and again "as a resistance." It may help for the therapist to challenge the patient's view in order to introduce a new point of view.

The therapist must avoid the complementary role which the patient's personality patterns call for as the patient tries to gain the analyst's approval. (The patient may be aware of his manipulative tendencies but the defensive aspect of these tendencies is generally unconscious. It is part of the patient's standard method of dealing with people.) The therapist's active involvement may become necessary. He may need to be more directive. Interpretations may be made as emphatic statements. A hoped-for result is that the patient see analysis as a new human experience.

Regan (1965), in an article entitled, "Brief Psychotherapy of Depression," is concerned with "tactics," a "circumscribed set of procedures aimed at a specific tactical goal." He advocates these tactical approaches in psychotherapy of depression:

1. Protection of patient. The therapist must anticipate the effects of his therapeutic efforts and the risk of patient's suicide.

2. Need for preparatory exploration. Since a conviction of hopelessness is a uniform feature of depression and leads to negativism about therapeutic efforts the therapist should arouse the patient into therapeutic activity by direct and aggressive questioning.

3. Interruption of the ruminative cycle. The psychotherapist prohibits the patient from engaging in activities in which he will fail and limits activities to a sphere in which he is sure the patient will succeed.

4. Use of physical therapy. For physical treatment to be lasting, the forces resulting in the depression must be eliminated simultaneously with the physical treatment.

5. Initiation of attitudinal change.

Bonime (1965) states that depression is a sick way of relating to other human beings. Characteristically, the depressive makes inordinate demands on others. Depressive living has a basic consistency pervading all its variations from neurotic sulking to psychotic mania, the elements of which are manipulativeness, aversion to influence, unwillingness to give gratification, hostility, and anxiety.

Bonime also states that the depressive's dreams show elements of anxiety and destructiveness, and reflect the way in which the patient reacts to people and the role he plays in producing the paralysis, anxiety, rage, and deprivations in his life. The therapist can help the patient to see possibilities of new choices and new consequences. The therapist must guard against subsidizing the depressive tactics of his patient. He must foster the patient's recognition of his role in bringing about his pain and the personal resources he (the patient) has for altering his practices.

SUPPORTIVE PSYCHOTHERAPY

Various methods used in the supportive treatment of depression have been described in detail by a number of authors (Appel, 1944; Campbell, 1953; Kraines, 1957; Ayd, 1961). There seems to be a consensus regarding supportive therapy and the discussion below reflects the generally accepted procedures.

REASSURANCE

The authors agree on the importance of stressing that depression is a self-limited disorder to counteract the patient's belief that he will never get better. Kraines gives his patients lengthy explanations, both of the factors involved in depression and of the course of the illness, and concludes, "The thing for you to remember is that this exhaustion can and will be overcome. You will need patience and you will need to cooperate. It won't be easy, it will take time; *but you will recover.*" (p. 409) He states that a majority of the patients are comforted, sustained, and encouraged by a straightforward explanation of their illness and by positive reassurance of their recovery.

Ayd emphasizes to his patients that although it may take weeks or months for complete recovery, they will feel progressively better and will not remain at their current level of depression. Ayd reports that, after recovery, many patients remark that their confidence in the physician's promise of recovery and his constant assurances prevented suicide and made their existence more tolerable.

I have found that optimistic statements about the outcome may encourage the patient to become more active and may help to neutralize the all-pervasive pessimism. In mild or moderate depressions such positive predictions may have a noticeable ameliorating effect but severely depressed patients may view these optimistic statements with skepticism and may fail to be influenced by them.

The therapist may often be of help in reassuring the patient about other misconceptions and worries, e.g., that he will be unable to provide for his family, that he will be unable to meet the minimal demands of living, or that his physical health is deteriorating rapidly. Through appropriate encouragement the therapist can often increase the patient's self-confidence and can counteract his feeling of helplessness.

Reassurance should be administered judiciously and with an awareness of the way it is construed by the patient. A bluff, hearty manner by the therapist may be interpreted as insincerity or insensitiveness by the patient and may increase his sense of hopelessness.

A depressed medical student told his therapist that he felt isolated and alone and that these symptoms meant to him that he was suffering from chronic schizophrenia. The therapist launched into a lengthy discussion of the difference between depression and schizophrenia. The patient's reaction to this was: "He doesn't understand me." The patient wanted to ventilate his worries and he felt that the therapist had cut him off with a premature reassurance. As a result he felt even more isolated.

Another technique that is often helpful in counteracting the patient's low self-esteem and hopeless feeling is a discussion of his positive achievements. If allowed to follow his inclinations, the patient is likely to dwell on past failures and traumatic experiences. The therapist, however, can foster a more realistic appraisal of the past and can raise the patient's self-evaluation by skillfully guiding him into describing his successes in detail.

VENTILATION AND CATHARSIS

It is worthwhile to draw the depressed patient into a discussion of the life situations and the relationships that are bothering him. Occasionally, the patient is helped by being able to express his problems and feelings to a permissive and understanding person. Some patients are inhibited in discussing their difficulties with their relatives or their closest friends, out of the fear that they will be criticized for complaining or because they anticipate humiliation from admitting they have emotional problems. They tend to equate emotional problems with weakness and character defects.

Some depressed patients experience considerable relief after ventilating their feelings and concerns to the therapist. The emotional release produced by crying occasionally produces a notable alleviation of the symptoms. Severely depressed patients, however, may react adversely to ventilation. After a discussion of their problems they may not only feel more overwhelmed and helpless but may, in addition, feel humiliated over having exposed themselves.

GUIDANCE AND ENVIRONMENTAL CHANGE

The need for some change in the patient's activities is often obvious and the therapist may draw on the therapeutic relationship to induce the patient to modify his routine. For instance, the therapist may act as a catalyst to redirect the patient from self-preoccupation to an interest in the outside world; he might suggest appropriate forms of recreational, manual, intellectual, or aesthetic activities.

Sometimes a change in the over-all pattern of living is helpful. For example, an ambitious businessman may be driving himself further into a depression by continuing his stressful activities and by denying himself any form of passive gratification. Since the patient might not reduce his absorption in business of his own volition the therapist may persuade him to take a vacation or to reduce his work load. When chronic marital tensions are contributing to a depression, marriage counselling or (in mild depressions) a period of separation from the spouse may be useful. Although these forms of reducing stress are often helpful in the *reactive* depressions, they must be used cautiously. Some depressed patients, particularly the severely depressed, may fare worse on vacation than if they continue with their regular occupations.

Severely depressed patients who are unable to continue with their usual occupation are often helped by being provided with a well-structured daily program. These patients experience a lack of organization, direction, and motivation. If left to their own inclinations they would stay in one place and brood. A daily program of scheduled hourly activities provides a tangible structure and tends to counteract the regressive, escapist wishes. The schedule, furthermore, helps these patients to mobilize constructive motivations and organize their thinking around external goals. In short, this program serves both as an integrative force and also as a distraction from the depressive brooding.

In recommending activities to a depressed patient, the therapist should attempt to gauge both the patient's tolerance for the stress involved and the probabilities of success. The particular task should not be too difficult or too time consuming. We have found that the successful completion of a task by depressed patients *significantly increases optimism, level of aspiration, and performance on subsequent tasks* (Loeb *et al.*, 1966).

Hospitalization is a more extreme form of environmental change and is definitely indicated when there is a serious suicidal risk. The hospital, furthermore, not only removes the patient from domestic stress but can provide a therapeutic regimen that is not available at home. A structured program of occupational therapy, recreational therapy, and group and individual psychotherapy has been shown to reduce the duration of psychotic depressions (Friedman *et al.*, 1966).

COGNITIVE (INSIGHT) PSYCHOTHERAPY

Cognitive psychotherapy is based on the theory elaborated by the author. In brief, the theory postulates that the depressed or depression-prone individual has certain idiosyncratic cognitive patterns (schemas) which may become activated either by specific stresses impinging on specific vulnerabilities or by overwhelming, nonspecific stresses. When the cognitive patterns are activated, they tend to dominate the individual's thinking and to produce the affective and motivational phenomena associated with depression. Cognitive psychotherapy may be used symptomatically during depressions to help the patient gain objectivity toward his automatic reactions and counteract them. During nondepressed periods, the therapy is designed to modify the idiosyncratic cognitive patterns to reduce the patient's vulnerability to future depressions.

The techniques consist of: a *macroscopic* or longitudinal approach, aimed at mapping out the patient's sensitivities, exaggerated or inappropriate reactions, and the cause-effect relationships between external events and internal discomfort; a *microscopic* or cross-sectional approach, focused on recognizing and evaluating specific cognitions; and the identification and modification of the misconceptions, superstitions, and syllogisms that lead to maladaptive reactions.

Although cognitive psychotherapy may be used in conjunction with supportive therapy during the depressive episodes, its major application is in the postdepressed period. During this period, the patient may have transient periods of feeling blue but for the most part is functioning well enough to be able to examine objectively his life patterns, his automatic thoughts, and his basic misconceptions. This approach is designed to produce changes in the cognitive organization to reduce the patient's vulnerability to future depressions.

I have also found cognitive psychotherapy effective in certain types of depressed patients *during* the depression; these are generally cases that would be classified as *reactive* rather than *endogenous* depressions. The characteristics of these patients are: (*a*) They are not severely ill; (*b*) The precipitation of the depression is related to a significant environmental event such as a disruption of a close interpersonal relationship or a serious financial reversal; and (*c*) The illness does not follow the typical U-shaped curve described in Chapter 3, namely, a continuous downward progression, then a flattening out, and then a continuous improvement. The depressed patient who is amenable to cognitive psychotherapy generally shows wide fluctuations during the course of a day and also from day to day. These fluctuations, moreover, are related to specific environmental events; positive experiences diminish and negative experiences increase the degree of depression.

DELINEATING THE MAJOR MALADAPTIVE PATTERNS

One of the first steps in the insight psychotherapy of the depressed patient is a survey of the life history data. In reviewing the patient's history of difficulties the therapist tries to identify the major patterns and sequences in the patient's life. It is generally possible to demonstrate to him that he responds *selectively* to certain types of experiences, i.e., he does not overreact to *every* type of difficult or unpleasant situation, but has a predilection to react excessively to *certain* events.

The therapist should attempt to reconstruct with the patient the stages in the development of his depression. These include the formation of maladaptive attitudes as the result of early experiences, the sensitization to particular types of stresses, and the precipitation of the depression as the result either of a gross traumatic event or of more insidious influences. By reviewing his history in this way, the patient is able to see his psychological disturbance in terms of specific problems rather than in terms of symptoms. The increased objectivity and understanding removes the mystery and may then provide a measure of mastery of the problems.

A patient suffering from intermittent depression reported that he had been feeling blue all day. At first he had no idea what had initiated his depressed feeling. He recalled that when he awoke he felt quite good. As he reported this he remembered that he started to feel somewhat below par when his wife did not get up to prepare breakfast for him. In recounting this episode he became visibly upset. He then realized that he had felt rejected by his wife's not getting up—even though he knew that she was very tired from having been up most of the night with their baby.

Tracing back his patterns of reaction, the patient recognized that he generally responded adversely whenever he did not get much attention. In grade school, for instance, where he was the teacher's pet, he felt hurt whenever the teacher praised another student or did not pay him a compliment. That he got more praise than any other student in the class did not relieve his feelings on the few occasions when he did not get praise. He recalled that later he felt similarly rejected when any of his close friends did not show the usual amount of warmth or camaraderie. Both his parents were very warm and indulgent people and he was aware of always wanting their approval (which he usually got) as well as that of almost everybody else he met.

In reviewing the cause-and-effect sequences, the patient recognized that he had a pattern of reading rejection into any situation in which he did not get preferential treatment. He could see the inappropriateness of this reaction. He realized, furthermore, that he depended on getting constant approval to maintain his sense of worthwhileness. When the approval was not forthcoming he was prone to react with hurt feelings. In applying this formulation to his reaction to his wife's not getting up in the morning, he realized that he had misinterpreted her behavior. As he said, "I guess I got it all wrong. She wasn't rejecting me. She simply was too tired to get up. I took it though as a sign of her not liking me and I felt bad about it."

Among the more common situations that produce disproportionate or inappropriate reactions in the depression-prone patient are: failing to reach a particular goal, being excluded from a group, being rejected by another person, receiving criticism, and not receiving expected approval, encouragement, or guidance. Although such situations might be expected to produce transient unpleasant reactions in the average person, they may produce prolonged feelings of disappointment or hopelessness in the depression-prone person.

By being primed in advance to recognize his typical overreaction, the patient is fortified when the specific stress occurs and he is less likely to be overwhelmed by it. It is generally possible for the therapist to point out the precise characteristics of the exaggerated reaction, viz., that the patient is reacting according to a repetitive pattern rather than to the specific features of the reality situation. The patient feels overwhelmed or hopeless, for example, not because the situation is overwhelming or insoluble but because he construes it that way. By referring to the past history, the therapist can demonstrate how the maladaptive pattern got started and was repeated on various occasions.

One woman, for instance, felt sad and unwanted whenever a friend or acquaintance had a party and did not invite her. Intense and prolonged feelings of rejection were aroused although she was very popular and was, in truth, invited to more parties than she had time to attend. We were able to date the onset of this rejection pattern to early adolescence when she entered junior high school. At that time she was excluded from various cliques that the other girls formed. She vividly remembered sitting alone in the cafeteria and thinking that she was socially undesirable and inferior to the other girls. In therapy, she was able to recognize that the rejection pattern was mobilized inappropriately in her adult life. Her concept, "I have no friends and nobody wants me," was no longer valid. Until it was pointed out that she was simply re-living a past experience, as it were, she tended to believe that not being invited to a party indicated that she did not really have any friends.

Neutralizing "Automatic Thoughts"

The second approach in insight therapy consists of the patient's focusing on his specific depression-generating cognitions. In the mild or moderately ill depressed patient, these thoughts are often at the periphery of awareness and require special focusing in order for the patient to recognize them. In psychoanalytical terminology, they would probably be regarded as preconscious. In the more severely ill depressed patient, however, these thoughts are at the center of the patient's phenomenal field and tend to dominate the thought content.

This kind of depression-generating cognition seems to be a highly condensed representation of more elaborate ideas. The ideas are apparently compressed into a kind of shorthand and a rather complicated thought occurs within a split second. Albert Ellis (1962) refers to these thoughts as "self-statements" or "internalized verbalizations." He explains these thoughts as "things that the patient tells himself." I have labeled these types of cognitions as *automatic thoughts.*

These self-statements or cognitions reflect the distortions that occur in the depressed state. As a result of these distortions, the patient experiences dysphoria. But when he can identify the distorted cognitions, and can acquire objectivity towards them and correct them, he can neutralize some of their pathogenic quality.

Pinpointing Depressive Cognitions

At the beginning of therapy the patient is generally aware only of the following sequence: events or stimulus → affect. He must be trained to fill in the link between the stimulus and the affect: stimulus → cognition → affect.

A patient, for example, reported that he felt blue every time. he made a mistake, and he could not understand why he should feel this way. He fully accepted the notion that there was nothing wrong in making mistakes and that it was an inevitable part of living. He was instructed to focus on his thoughts the next time he felt an unpleasant affect in connection with making a mistake. At the next interview he reported the observation that whenever he made a mistake he would think "I'm a dope," or "I never do anything right," or "How can anybody be so dumb." After having one of these thoughts he would become depressed. By becoming aware of the self-criticisms, however, he was able to recognize how unreasonable they were. This recognition seemed to remove the sting from his blue reactions.

The automatic thoughts not only bear a relationship to unpleasant affect but also bear a relationship to many of the other phenomena of depression. Loss of motivation, for example, is based on such ideas as "I won't be able to do it," or "If I do this, I will only feel worse."

As the patient becomes more adept at recognizing the precise wording of his automatic thoughts, he is less influenced by them. He can view them as though from a distance and can assess their validity. The processes of recognition and distancing are the initial steps in neutralizing the automatic thoughts.

Identifying Idiosyncratic Content

As the patient gains experience in recognizing his cognitions he becomes ready to identify the common themes among the cognitions that produce an unpleasant feeling. In order to help him to categorize his cognitions, I generally point out the major depressive themes, such as deprivation, self-reproach, or sense of inferiority. It is important to emphasize that of the innumerable ways in which he can interpret his life experiences he tends to perseverate in a few stereotyped interpretations or explanations; he may, for example, repeatedly interpret any interpersonal difficulty or dissension as indicating his own deficiency. It is also important to point out to him how these depressive cognitions actually represent distortions of reality.

It is often difficult for the patient to accept the idea that his interpretations are incorrect, or at least inaccurate. In fact, the more depressed the patient is, the more difficult it is for him to regard the depressive cognitions with any degree of objectivity.

Recognizing Formal Characteristics of Cognitions

To increase the patient's objectivity towards his cognitions and to help him evaluate them, it is often helpful to point out some of the characteristics of the cognitions. This not only helps him to identify them, but it also gives him a chance to question their authenticity.

It is often valuable to make a distinction for the patient between "two types of thinking." The first type is the *higher-level* type of thinking that involves judgment, weighing of the evidence, and consideration of alternative explanations (secondary process). The *lower-level* form of cognition, in contrast, tends to be relatively rapid and does not seem to involve any complicated logical processes (primary process).

One of the characteristics of the lower-level cognitions is that they tend to be *automatic*. They arise as if by reflex and are generally not the result of deliberation or careful reasoning. A patient observed that when she approached a task (preparing a meal, writing a letter, making a phone call) she immediately had the thought, "I can't do it." When she focused her attention on this thought, she recognized its arbitrariness and she was able to assume some detachment towards it. After the patient has been successful in specifying the idiosyncratic cognitions generated by certain specific situations, he is in a better position to prepare himself to deal with them when they arise.

Another important characteristic of the depressive cognitions is their *involuntary* quality. In the more severe cases, particularly, it is apparent that these cognitions continuously invade the phenomenal field and the patient has little power to ward them off or to focus his attention on something else. Even when he is determined to think rationally about a situation and to make an objective judgment he is apt to be diverted by the relentless intrusion of the depressive cognitions. This perseverating and compelling quality of the depressive cognitions may be so strong as to make any form of insight therapy fruitless at this stage.

In the less severely ill patient, the recognition of the involuntary aspect of the cognitions helps to drive home that they are not the result of any deliberation or reasoning. The patient is able to look upon them as a kind of obsession that intrudes onto his more rational thinking but that does not have to be given any particular truth value.

One of the crucial characteristics of these cognitions in terms of psychotherapy is that they seem *plausible* to the patient. Even normal people tend to accept the validity of their thoughts without subjecting them to any kind of careful scrutiny. The problem is compounded for the depressed patient because the idiosyncratic cognitions seem especially plausible or real. At times the more incongruous these cognitions may appear to the therapist the more plausible they may seem to the patient. The more reasonable the thought seems to be, the greater is the affective reaction. The converse also seems to be true; the more intense the affective state, the more credible the depressive cognitions are to the patient. When the intensity of the affect is reduced through antidepressant drugs, there is a diminution in the compelling quality of the cognitions. This seems to indicate an interaction between cognition and affect.

Distinguishing "Ideas" from "Facts"

After the patient becomes experienced in recognizing the idiosyncratic content and other characteristics of the cognitions, the therapeutic work consists of training him to evaluate their validity or accuracy. This procedure consists essentially of the application of the rules of evidence and logic to the cognitions and the consideration of alternative explanations or interpretations by the patient.

In examining the validity of a cognition, the patient first must learn to make a distinction between thinking and believing; i.e., simply because he *thinks* something does not, *ipso facto*, mean he should *believe it*. Despite the often apparent sophistication of the patient it is necessary to point out that thoughts are not equivalent to external reality, and, no matter how convincing they may seem, they should not be accepted unless validated by some objective procedure.

A patient, for instance, had the thought that his girlfriend no longer liked him. Instead of treating this notion as a hypothesis he accepted it as an actuality. He then used this notion to explain recent differences in his girlfriend's behavior and thus fortified his acceptance of the idea. The goal of therapy is to help the patient shift from this type of deductive analysis of experience to more inductive procedures. By checking his observations, by taking into account all the data, and by considering other hypotheses to explain the events, he is less prone to equate his automatic thoughts with reality.

Checking Observations

The validation of the patient's interpretations and judgments depends on checking the accuracy and completeness of the initial observations. On reflection, the patient frequently discovers that either his original impression of a situation was distorted or that he jumped to a conclusion too quickly and thus ignored or rejected salient details that were not compatible with that conclusion. A professor, for example, was downcast and complained that he was "slipping" because "nobody showed up" for a lecture. On re-examining the evidence, he realized that this was his initial impression, but that in actuality most of the seats in the lecture hall were filled. Having made an incorrect preliminary judgment, he had failed to correct it until he was helped to re-examine the evidence.

A woman told me she had "made a fool out of myself" in a job interview the day before. She felt humiliated and downcast up to the time of our appointment. I then inquired "What *actually happened* in the interview?" As she recounted the details of the interview, she realized that she had handled it rather well and that her negative judgment was based on only one short portion of the interview.

Responding to Depressive Cognitions

Once the patient has established that a particular cognition is invalid it is important for him (or the therapist) to neutralize its effects by stating precisely why it is inaccurate, inappropriate, or invalid. By verbalizing the reasons that the idea was erroneous, the patient is able to reduce the intensity and frequency of the idea as well as of the accompanying affect.

A depressed patient, for instance, found that no matter how fastidiously she cleaned a drawer or closet she thought that it was still dirty. This made her feel discouraged until she began to counter the thought with the following rebuttal: "I'm a good housekeeper—which I know and other people have told me. There's absolutely no sign of dirt. It's just as clean as it ever is when I'm not depressed. There may be a few specks of dust but that's not dirt." On another occasion, when she started to prepare a roast, she had the thought, "I won't be able to do it." She reasoned the problem through and verbalized to herself, "I've done this many times before. I may be a little slower than usual because I'm depressed but I know what to do and if I think it out step-by-step there's no reason why I can't do it." She felt heartened after this and finished preparing the meal.

It is often helpful for the patient to label the particular paralogical mechanisms involved in the depressive cognition, e.g., overgeneralization, arbitrary inference, selective abstraction, or magnification. If he can say to himself, "I'm taking this out of context," or "I'm jumping to conclusions," or "I'm exaggerating," he may be able to reduce the power of the depressive cognition.

Weighing Alternative Explanations

Another method of neutralizing the inaccurate negative interpretations is the consideration of alternative explanations. For instance, a patient, who was exceptionally personable and popular, would characteristically interpret any reduction of enthusiasm toward her as a sign of rejection and also as evidence that she was unlikeable. After some training in dealing with her idiosyncratic cognitions, she reported the following incident. She was conversing on the telephone with an old friend when the friend said she had to hang up because she had a beauty parlor appointment. The patient's immediate thought was, "She doesn't like me," and she felt sad and disappointed. Applying the technique of alternative explanations, she countered with the following: "Marjorie has been my friend for many years. She has always shown that she likes me. I know she has a beauty parlor appointment today and that is obviously the reason why she had to hang up." Her initial interpretation was part of a stereotyped pattern and excluded the proffered explanation. When the patient reviewed the episode and considered the possible explanations she was able to accept her friend's explanation as more probable than her automatic interpretations.

Validating Basic Premises

Although the technique just described deals directly with the specific cognitions, the operation to be described in this section is directed towards the patient's underlying chronic misconceptions, prejudices, and superstitions about himself and his world. Allied to these are the assumptions basic to the way the individual sets goals, assesses and modifies his behavior, and explains adverse occurrences; these assumptions underlie the injunctions, debasements, criticisms, punitiveness, and blame that the patient directs to himself. The aim to modify these chronic attitudes and patterns (schemas) is based on the thesis that they partly determine the content of the individual's cognitions. It should follow that a basic modification or attenuation of these schemas would modify the way he organizes and interprets specific experiences, as well as how he sets his goals and goes about achieving them.

The content of the chronic attitudes may be readily inferred from the examination of the recurrent themes in the patient's cognitive responses to particular situations and in his free associations (themes of personal deficiency, debility, and hopelessness). Further information about his basic premises and assumptions may be obtained by asking him either what he bases a particular conclusion on, or his reasons for a specific judgment. An inquiry into his values, opinions, and beliefs will yield additional data. Some idea of the schemas used in approaching his problems or in attaining goals may be obtained by an examination of his self-instructions and self-reproaches. One of the useful features of this approach is that it attempts to correct the major premises or assumptions that form the basis for the deductive thinking. Since the predominance of deductive (as opposed to inductive) thinking is an important determinant of the cognitive distortions in depression, any correction of the invalid major premises will tend to reduce the erroneous conclusions.

Illustrative of the typical assumptions and premises underlying the cognitive distortions in depression are ideas such as the following: "It is very bad to make a mistake." "If anything goes wrong, it's my fault." "I'm basically unlucky and bring bad luck to myself and everybody else." "If I don't continue to make a lot of money, I will go bankrupt." "I really am quite stupid and my academic success is the result of clever faking." "Trouble with constipation is a sign of disintegration."

Let us say that a patient reports, "Everything I did today was wrong;" or "Everybody has been pushing me around;" or "I'm getting uglier every day." The therapist may review with the patient the evidence for these conclusions and may attempt to demonstrate that the ideas are exaggerations or frank misinterpretations. Often, however, the ideas are so strong that the patient cannot even contemplate the possibility that they could be inaccurate. In such cases, the force of the ideas may be weakened by dissecting the network of underlying assumptions.

A depressed woman of 40 had strong suicidal wishes. She justified these as follows: "What's the use of living. I've got to die some time anyhow. I'm just prolonging something that's deteriorating. It's a losing battle so I might as well get out now before I've deteriorated completely." Rebuttals to the effect she was still relatively young, attractive, and healthy and that she still had many potential years of happiness did not influence her thinking. She clung to the notion that she was decaying and that, if she lived, she would soon experience the horror of physical disintegration.

One day, in looking in the mirror, she observed that the image appeared to be that of her mother during her terminal illness. She turned her head in disgust and felt more depressed. Although she realized that the reflection was hers, not her mother's, she could not shake the belief that she had already deteriorated so much that she now looked like her dying mother.

Drawing on this information, I said to the patient, "Your whole idea of quitting life is based on one premise: You believe that you are following in your mother's footsteps. You got the notion when she was dying that when you reached her age (40 years) you would start to have strokes and would go to pieces. The truth of the matter is that all our tests have shown that your physical health is perfect. Your mother had severe diabetes since childhood and she became blind and had her strokes as a complication of the diabetes. However, you don't have diabetes and, in fact, you don't have any physical disease."

I explained to the patient how she had identified herself with her mother and how this formed the basis for the premise that she was starting to deteriorate. She had, without fully realizing it, adopted the formula: getting old (i.e. more than 40 years) equals becoming deteriorated and ugly. By pinpointing this formula, we were able to discuss its validity. As she was able to see the arbitrariness of this equation, her ideas that she was ugly and deteriorating started to fade as did her suicidal wishes.

Sometimes the patient can see the fallacy of his basic assumptions without any difficulty. However, the simple acknowledgement of their irrationality may not change them. They may continue to be manifest in repetitive automatic thoughts. It is often necessary to examine the invalid assumptions repeatedly and to encourage the patient to state the reasons they are invalid. Sometimes, I direct the patient to specify the argument in favor of the invalid assumption and then the argument against it. At other times I offer the argument supporting an invalid assumption and induce the patient to supply the rebuttal.

A scientist felt sad and empty whenever he failed to get recognition for his performance. We were able to establish that he had a set of interlocking premises: "It is of utmost importance that I become famous. The only gratification I can get out of life is by being acclaimed by everybody. If I do not achieve fame, then my life is worthless and meaningless." If these premises were correct, then it would be inevitable that he would feel ungratified and empty when he missed out on recognition. If they were invalid, then they could be modified and he would be less subject to feelings of desolation when he failed to get recognition.

To test the validity of these assumptions, I presented the following argument. "If these premises are true, we would expect the following to happen. One, that you never obtain gratification from anything except recognition. Two, that recognition has brought you gratification. Three, that nothing in life means anything or is worth anything to you except fame."

Upon hearing this argument, the patient was quick to provide a rebuttal. "I *have* gotten pleasure from lots of things that don't involve recognition. I enjoy my family and friends. I get a lot of satisfaction from reading and listening to classical records and going to concerts. Also I really do enjoy my work and would like what I'm doing even if I did not get any recognition at all. Besides, when I do get recognition, I don't get much feeling of satisfaction from it. Actually, I find that personal relationships are more satisfying than getting an article published."

After many discussions of this nature, the exaggerated emphasis on recognition was reduced, and the patient found that he was able to get more enjoyment out of his work because he was no longer continually worried about recognition. Furthermore, he was able to enjoy his nonprofessional activities more because activities not directed towards achieving fame no longer were regarded as a waste of time.

MODIFYING MOOD BY INDUCED FANTASIES

Some depressed patients report spontaneous fantasies (daydreams), which have a gloomy content such as deprivation, personal inadequacy, and thwarting. When he contemplates an event in the near or distant future, the patient has a pictorial image of a negative outcome.

A depressed woman sat down to prepare her list of items to be purchased at a grocery store. She then experienced the following fantasy, which she later reported to me: "I went into the supermarket with my marketing list. I went from counter to counter and I couldn't find what I wanted. I then noticed that people were looking at me peculiarly as though they thought I was crazy. I felt so humiliated I had to leave without buying anything." As a result she did not go to the market that day.

It is noteworthy that while she was having this fantasy, the patient experienced intense humiliation as though the fantasied event was occurring in reality. In an attempt to help her deal with the expectation of frustration and humiliation, I asked her to imagine the scene in the supermarket again. This time she felt less humiliation. After imagining the same scene three more times, she no longer felt any unpleasant affect in association with the fantasy. She remarked, "I can see that I was really exaggerating the problem in my daydream." Following this interview, the patient was able to do her marketing without any difficulty.

This example illustrates that a patient may react to his fantasies in much the same way that he reacts to his automatic thoughts. The patient may be trained to deal therapeutically with his fantasies in much the same way as he can deal with maladaptive ideas of a verbal nature.

By having the patient repeat the depressive fantasy during the therapy session, the therapist can help him gain greater objectivity towards the actual real life situation. This kind of *rehearsal* may then enable the patient to undertake a task that he had previously avoided.

Sometimes spontaneous modification of the content of the fantasy may be achieved by simple repetition of the fantasy. A patient was feeling pessimistic about his job and had a fantasy on the way to my office: "I went into my superior's office with a suggestion. He got very angry with me. I felt I had stepped beyond the proper bounds." The feeling that accompanied this fantasy was discouragement and humiliation. When I asked him to imagine the scene again, he experienced a repetition of the same unpleasant affects.

I then asked the patient to imagine the scene once more. This time the fantasy was as follows: "My boss was interested in what I had to say. He wanted more information. I felt that there was a mutual interchange between two professionals." The affect accompanying this fantasy was pleasant. Concomitantly, the patient's generally pessimistic mood about the anticipated events of the day lifted and he went to work feeling more optimistic and self-confident. The actual outcome of his interaction with his superior was similar to that in the pleasant fantasy.

I have found in other cases that it has been possible to alleviate pessimism by inducing the patient to have more realistic fantasies about anticipated events. Another technique of combatting the sense of inadequacy or deprivation is to suggest that the patient recall in pictorial form certain past successes or gratifications. Upon revivifying the past memories, the patient often experiences a sense of gratification that persists for the rest of the day.

The technique of fantasy induction serves much the same purpose as examination of the maladaptive self-verbalizations. By examining his gloomy fantasies, the patient is able to loosen their grip on him, to reality test them, and to consider more favorable outcomes. Moreover, the induction of pleasant fantasies helps to neutralize his sadness and pessimism.

Bibliography

ABRAHAM, K. (1911): "Notes on the Psychoanalytic Investigation and Treatment of Manic-Depressive Insanity and Allied Conditions," in *Selected Papers on Psychoanalysis*. New York, Basic Books, 1960, pp. 137–156.

AMERICAN PSYCHIATRIC ASSOCIATION (1952): *Diagnostic and Statistical Manual: Mental Disorders*. Washington, D.C.

APPEL, K.E. (1944): "Psychiatric Therapy," in *Personality and the Behavior Disorders*, ed. by Hunt, J. New York, Ronald Press, vol. II, pp. 1107–1163.

ARIETI, S. (1962): The psychotherapeutic approach to depression. *Amer. J. Psychother. 61:*397–406.

ASCHER, E. (1952): A criticism of the concept of neurotic depression. *Amer. J. Psychiat. 108:*901–908.

ASTRUP, C., FOSSUM, A., and HOLMBOE, F. (1959): A follow-up study of 270 patients with acute affective psychoses. *Acta Psychiat. Scand. Suppl. 135.*

AYD, F.J., Jr. (1958): Drug-induced depression—fact or fallacy. *New York J. Med. 58:*354–356.

AYD, F.J., JR. (1961): *Recognizing the Depressed Patient*. New York, Grune & Stratton.

BECK, A.T. (1961): A systematic investigation of depression. *Compr. Psychiat. 2:* 162–170.

BECK, A.T. and VALIN, S. (1953): Psychotic depressive reactions in soldiers who accidentally killed their buddies. *Amer. J. Psychiat. 110:*347–353.

BECK, A.T., WARD, C.H., MENDELSON, M., MOCK, J.E., and ERBAUGH, J.K. (1962): Reliability of psychiatric diagnoses: 2. A study of consistency of clinical judgments and ratings. *Amer. J. Psychiat. 119:*351–357.

BEERS, C.W. (1928): *A Mind That Found Itself: An Autobiography*. Garden City, N.Y., Doubleday.

BLEULER, E. (1911): *Dementia Praecox or the Group of Schizophrenia*, trans. by Zinken, J. New York, Internat. Univ. Press, 1950.

BLEULER, E. (1924). *Textbook of Psychiatry*, trans. by Brill, A.A. New York, Macmillan.

BOND, E.D. and MORRIS, H.H., JR. (1954): Results of treatment in psychoses— with a control series: III. Manic-depressive reactions. *Amer. J. Psychiat. 110:* 881–887.

BONIME, W (1965): A psychotherapeutic approach to depression. *Contemporary Psychoanalysis 2:*48–53.

BOYLE, H. (1930): Discussion on the diagnosis and treatment of the milder forms of the manic-depressive psychosis. *Proc. Roy. Soc. Med. 23:*881–892.

BRADLEY, J.J. (1963): Severe localized pain associated with the depressive syndrome. *Brit. J. Psychiat. 109:* 741–745.

BRIGHT, T. (1586): "Melancholy and the Conscience of Sinne," in *Three Hundred Years of Psychiatry 1535–1860,* ed. by Hunter, R., and MacAlpine, I. London, Oxford, 1963, pp. 36–40.

BUZZARD, E.F. (1930): Discussion of the diagnosis and treatment of the milder forms of the manic-depressive psychosis. *Proc. Roy. Soc. Med. 23:*881-883.

CAMPBELL, J.D. (1953): *Manic-Depressive Disease.* Philadelphia, Lippincott.

CANDOLLE, A.P. DE (1816): *Essai sur les propriétés medicales des plantes, comparées avec leurs formes extérieures et leur classification naturelle.* Paris, Crochard.

CARNEY, M.W.P., ROTH, M., and GARSIDE, R.F. (1965): The diagnosis of depressive syndromes and the prediction of E.C.T. response. *Brit. J. Psychiat. 3:*659–674.

CASSIDY, W.L., FLANAGAN, N.B., and SPELLMAN, M. (1957): Clinical observations in manic-depressive disease: a quantitative study of 100 manic-depressive patients and 50 medically sick controls. *J. Amer. Med. Ass. 164:*1535–1546.

CASTELNUOVO-TEDESCO, P. (1961): *Depressions in Patients with Physical Disease.* Cranbury, N.J., Wallace Laboratories.

CHENEY, C.O. (1934): *Outlines for Psychiatric Examinations.* Albany, New York State Dept. of Mental Hygiene.

CLARK, J.A. and MALLET, B.A. (1963): Follow-up study of schizophrenia and depression in young adults. *Brit. J. Psychiat. 109:*491–499.

COLE, J.O. (1964): Therapeutic efficacy of antidepressant drugs. *J. Amer. Med. Ass. 190:*448–455.

CRICHTON-MILLER, H. (1930): Discussion of the diagnosis and treatment of the milder forms of the manic-depressive psychosis. *Proc. Roy. Soc. Med. 23:*883–886.

CRONHOLM, B. and MOLANDER, L. (1964): Memory disturbances after electroconvulsive therapy: 5. Conditions one month after a series of treatments. *Acta Psychiat. Scand. 40:*212.

DAVIS, J. (1965): Efficacy of tranquilizing and antidepressant drugs. *Arch. Gen. Psychiat. (Chicago) 13:*552–572.

DENISON, R. and YASKIN, J.C. (1944): Medical and surgical masquerades of the depressed state. *Penn. Med. J. 47:*703–707.

DOVENMUEHLE, R.H. and VERWOERDT, A. (1962): Physical illness and depressive symptomatology. I. Incidence of depressive symptoms in hospitalized cardiac patients. *J. Amer. Geriat. Soc. 10:*932–947.

DUNLOP, E. (1965): Use of antidepressants and stimulants. *Mod. Treatm. 2:*543–568.

ELLIS, A. (1962): *Reason and Emotion in Psychotherapy.* New York, Lyle Stuart.

FLEMING, G.W. (1933): The revision of the classification of mental disorders. *J. Ment. Sci. 79:*753.

FOULDS, G.A. (1960): Psychotic depression and age. *J. Ment. Sci. 106:*1394.

FRIEDMAN, A.S., COWITZ, B., COHEN, H.W., and GRANICK, S. (1963): Syndromes and themes of psychotic depression: a factor analysis. *Arch. Gen. Psychiat. (Chicago) 9:*504–509.

FRIEDMAN, A.S., GRANICK, S., COHEN, H.W., and COWITZ, B. (1966): Imipramine (Tofranil) vs. placebo in hospitalized psychotic depressives. *J. Psychiat. Res. 4:*13–36.

GIBSON, R.W. (1963): Psychotherapy of manic-depressive states. *Psychiat. Res. Rep. Amer. Psychiat. Ass. 17:*91–102.

GILLESPIE, R.D. (1929): Clinical differentiation of types of depression. *Guy Hosp. Rep. 79:*306–344.

GRINKER, R., MILLER, J., SABSHIN, M., NUNN, R., and NUNNALLY, J. (1961): *The Phenomena of Depressions.* New York, Hoeber.

HARROWES, W. McC. (1933): The depressive reaction types. *J. Ment. Sci. 79:* 235–246.

HINSIE, L. and CAMPBELL, R. (1960): *Psychiatric Dictionary,* 3rd ed. London, Oxford Univ. Press.

HOCH, A. (1921): *Benign Stupors: A Study of a New Manic-Depressive Reaction Type.* New York, Macmillan.

HOCH, P.H. (1953): Discussion of D.E. Cameron, "A Theory of Diagnosis," in *Current Problems in Psychiatric Diagnosis,* ed. by Hoch, P.H., and Zubin, J. New York, Grune & Stratton, pp. 46–50.

HOCH, P.H. and RACHLIN, H.L. (1941): An evaluation of manic-depressive psychosis in the light of follow-up studies. *Amer. J. Psychiat. 97:*831–843.

HOLMBERG, G. (1963): "Biological Aspects of Electro-convulsive Therapy," in *International Review of Neurobiology,* ed. by Pfeiffer, C., and Smythies, J. New York, Academic Press, vol. 5, pp. 389–406.

HOPKINSON, G. (1963): Onset of affective illness. *Psychiat. Neurol. (Basel) 146:* 133–140.

HOPKINSON, G. (1965): The prodromal phase of the depressive psychosis. *Psychiat. Neurol. (Basel) 149:*1–6.

HORDERN, A. (1965): The antidepressant drugs. *New Eng. J. Med. 272:*1159–1169.

HUSTON, P.E. and LOCHER, L.M. (1948). Manic-depressive psychosis: course when treated with electric shock. *Arch. Neurol. Psychiat. 60:*37–48.

JELLIFFE, S.E. (1931): Some historical phases of the manic-depressive synthesis. *Ass. Res. Nerv. Ment. Proc. 11:*3–47.

KALINOWSKI, L.B. and HOCH, P.H. (1961): *Somatic Treatments in Psychiatry.* New York, Grune & Stratton.

KENNEDY, F. (1944): The neuroses: related to the manic-depressive constitution. *Med. Clin. of N. Amer. 28:*452–466.

KENNEDY, F. and WIESEL, B. (1946): The clinical nature of "manic-depressive equivalents" and their treatment. *Trans. Amer. Neurol. Ass. 71:*96–101.

KILOH, L.G., and GARSIDE, R.F. (1963): The independence of neurotic depression and endogenous depression. *Brit. J. Psychiat. 109:*451–463.

KLERMAN, G.L., and COLE, J.O. (1965): Clinical pharmacology of imipramine and related antidepressant compounds. *Pharmacol. Rev. 17:*101–141.

KLINE, N. (1964): Practical management of depression. *J. Amer. Med. Ass. 190:* 732–740.

KRAEPELIN, E. (1913): "Manic-Depressive Insanity and Paranoia," in *Textbook of Psychiatry*, trans. by Barclay, R.M. Edinburgh, Livingstone.

KRAINES, S.H. (1957): *Mental Depressions and Their Treatment.* New York, Macmillan.

KRAL, V.A. (1958): Masked depression in middle-aged men. *Canad. Med. Ass. J. 79:*1–5.

KREITMAN, N., SAINSBURY, P., MORRISSEY, J., TOWERS, J., and SCRIVENER, J. (1961): The reliability of psychiatric assessment: an analysis. *Brit. J. Psychiat. 107:*887–908.

LANGE, J. (1926): Über Melancholie. *Z. Neurol. Psychiat. 101:*293–319.

LEHMAN, H.E. (1959): Psychiatric concepts of depression: nomenclature and classification. *Canad. Psychiat. Ass. J. Suppl. 4:*S1–S12.

LEWIS, A. (1934): Melancholia: a clinial survey of depressive states. *J. Ment. Sci. 80:*277–378.

LEWIS, A. (1938): States of depression: their clinical and aetiological differentiation. *Brit. Med. J. 2:*875–883.

LEWIS, N.D.C. and PIOTROWSKI, Z.S. (1954): "Clinical Diagnosis of Manic-Depressive Psychosis," in *Depression*, ed. by Hoch, P.H., and Zubin, J. New York, GRUNE & STRATTON, pp. 25–38.

LOEB, A., BECK, A.T., DIGGORY, J.C., and TUTHILL, R. (1966): The effects of success and failure on mood, motivation, and performance as a function of predetermined level of depression. Unpublished study.

LUNDQUIST, G. (1945): Prognosis and course in manic-depressive psychoses. *Acta Psychiat. Neurol. Suppl. 35.*

MAPOTHER, E. (1926). Discussion on manic-depressive psychosis. *Brit. Med. J. 2:* 872–876.

MENDELS, J. (1965): Electroconvulsive therapy and depression. *Brit. J. Psychiat. 3:*675–681.

MEYER, A. (1908): "The Problems of Mental Reaction Types," in *The Collected Papers of Adolf Meyer*. Baltimore, Md., Johns Hopkins Press, 1951, vol. 2, pp. 591–603.

MICHAEL, R.P. and GIBBONS, J.L. (1963): "Interrelationships between the Endocrine System and Neuropsychiatry," in *International Review of Neurobiology*, ed. by Pfeifer, C., and Smythies, J. New York, Academic Press.

MOSS, L.M. and HAMILTON, D.M. (1956): The psychotherapy of the suicidal patient. *Amer. J. Psychiat. 112:*814–820.

MOTTO, J.A. (1965): Suicide attempts: a longitudinal view. *Arch. Gen. Psychiat. (Chicago) 13:*516–520.

MACDONALD, J.M. (1964): Suicide and homicide by automobile. *Amer. J. Psychiat. 121:*366–370.

NUSSBAUM, K. and MICHAUX, W.W. (1963): Response to humor in depression: a prediction and evaluation of patient change? *Psychiat. Quart. 37:*527–539.

OSWALD, I., BERGER, R.J., JARAMILLO, R.A., KEDDIE, K.M.G., OLLEY, P.C., and PLUNKETT, G.B. (1963): Melancholia and barbiturates: a controlled EEG, body and eye movement study of sleep. *Brit. J. Psychiat. 109:*66–78.

PARTRIDGE, M. (1949): Some reflections on the nature of affective disorders arising from the results of prefrontal leucotomy. *J. Ment. Sci. 95:*795–825.

PASKIND, H.A. (1929): Brief attacks of manic-depressive depression. *Arch. Neurol. Psychiat. 22:*123–134.

PASKIND, H.A. (1930a): Manic-depressive psychosis as seen in private practice: sex and age incidence of first attacks. *Arch. Neurol. Psychiat. 23:*152–158.

PASKIND, H.A. (1930b): Manic-depressive psychosis in private practice: length of attack and length of interval. *Arch. Neurol. Psychiat. 23:*789–794.

PICHOT, P. and LEMPÉRIÈRE, T. (1964): Analyse factorielle d'un questionnaire d'autoévaluation des symptomes dépressifs. *Rev. Psychol. Appl. 14:*15–29.

POKORNY, A.D. (1964): Suicide rates in various psychiatric disorders. *J. Nerv. Ment. Dis. 139:*499–506.

POLLACK, H.M. (1931): Prevalence of manic-depressive psychosis in relation to sex, age, environment, nativity, and race. *Res. Publ. Ass. Res. Nerv. Ment. Dis. 11:*655–667.

RADO, S. (1928): The problem of melancholia. *Int. J. Psychoanal. 9:*420–438.

REGAN, P.F. (1965): Brief psychotherapy of depression. *Amer. J. Psychiat. 122:* 28–32.

RENNIE, T. (1942): Prognosis in manic-depressive psychoses. *Amer. J. Psychiat. 98:*801–814.

RIDDELL, S.A. (1963): The therapeutic efficacy of ECT. *Arch. Gen. Psychiat. (Chicago) 8:*546–556.

ROBINS, E., GASSNER, S., KAYES, J., WILKINSON, R.H., and MURPHY, G.E. (1959): The communication of suicidal intent: a study of 134 consecutive cases of successful (completed) suicide. *Amer. J. Psychiat. 115:*724–733.

SANDIFER, M.G., JR., WILSON, I.C., and GREEN, L. (1966): The two-type thesis of depressive disorders. *Amer. J. Psychiat. 123:*93–97.

SANDLER, S. (1948): Depression masking organic diseases and organic diseases masking depression. *J. Med. Soc. New Jersey 45:*108–110.

SAUL, L.J. (1947): *Emotional Maturity.* Philadelphia, Lippincott.

SCHWAB, J.J., BIALOW, M., and HOLZER, C. (1967): A comparison of two rating scales for depression. *J. Clin. Psychol. 23:*94–96.

SCHWAB, J.J., CLEMMONS, R.S., BIALOW, B., DUGGAN, V., and DAVIS, B. (1965): A study of the somatic symptomatology of depression in medical inpatients. *Psychosomatics 6:*273–277.

SIMONSON, M. (1964): Phenothiazine depressive reaction. *J. Neuropsychiat. 5:* 259–265.

SORENSON, A. and STROMGREN, E. (1961): Frequency of depressive states within geographically delimited population groups. *Acta Psychiat. Scand. Suppl. 162:* 62–68.

STEEN, R. (1933): Prognosis in manic-depressive psychoses: with report of factors studied in 493 patients. *Psychiat. Quart. 7:*419–429.

STENGEL, E. (1962): Recent research into suicide and attempted suicide. *Amer. J. Psychiat. 118:*725–727.

STENSTEDT, A. (1952): A study in manic-depressive psychosis: clinical, social, and genetic investigations. *Acta Psychiat. Scand. Suppl. 79.*

STRECKER, E.A., APPEL, K.E., EYMAN, E.V., FARR, C.B., LA MAR, N.C., PALMER,

H.D., and SMITH, L.H. (1931): The prognosis in manic-depressive psychosis. *Res. Publ. Ass. Res. Nerv. Ment. Dis. 11:*471–538.

TEMOCHE, A., PUGH, T.F., and MACMAHON, B. (1964): Suicide rates among current and former mental institution patients. *J. Nerv. Ment. Dis. 136:*124–130.

UNITED STATES WAR DEPARTMENT (1945): Tech. Bull. Med. 203. *Nomenclature and Method of Recording Diagnosis.* October 19, 1945.

VON HAGEN, K.O. (1957): Chronic intolerable pain; discussion of its mechanism and report of 8 cases treated with electroshock. *J. Amer. Med. Ass. 165:*773–777.

WARD, C.H., BECK, A.T., MENDELSON, M., MOCK, J.E., and ERBAUGH, J.K. (1962): The psychiatric nomenclature: reasons for diagnostic disagreement. *Arch. Gen. Psychiat. (Chicago) 7:*198–205.

WATTS, C.A. (1957): The mild endogenous depression. *Brit. Med. J. 1:*4–8.

WECHSLER, H., GROSSER, G., and GREENBLATT, M. (1965): Research evaluating antidepressant medications on hospitalized mental patients: a survey of published reports during a five year period. *J. Nerv. Ment. Dis. 141:*231–239.

WESSMAN, A.E. and RICKS, D.F. (1966): *Mood and Personality.* New York, Holt.

WEXBERG, E. (1928): Zur Klinik und Pathogenese der leichten Depressionzustände. *Z. Neurol. Psychiat. 112:*549–574.

WHEAT, W.D. (1960): Motivational aspects of suicide in patients during and after psychiatric treatment. *Southern Med. J. 53:*273–278.

WILSON, D.C. (1955): Dynamics and psychotherapy of depression. *J. Amer. Med. Ass. 158:*151–153.

WINOKUR, G. and PITTS, F.N. (1965): Affective disorder. IV. A family history study of prevalances, sex differences, and possible genetic factors. *J. Psychiat. Res. 3:*113–123.

YASKIN, J.C. (1931): Nervous symptoms as earliest manifestations of carcinoma of the pancreas. *J. Amer. Med. Ass. 96:*1664–1668.

YASKIN, J.C., WEISENBERG, T.H., and PLEASANTS, H. (1931): Neuropsychiatric counterfeits of organic visceral disease. *J. Amer. Med. Ass. 97:*1751–1756.

Pennsylvania Paperbacks